Praise for
A Is for Attitude

"Patricia Russell-McCloud is the greatest orator of our time. Now she brings the same power and magic of her speeches to the printed page in *A Is for Attitude*. It is a life-changing and inspirational work, an indispensable guide to living beautifully and with satisfaction."

—Les Brown, speaker, author of
Live Your Dreams and *It's Not Over Until You Win*

"Patricia Russell-McCloud is not only a visionary leader and great communicator, she also has that rare ability to capture the essence of great ideas and communicate them with clarity, simplicity, and power. *A Is for Attitude* is a written reflection of Patricia's gifts. For those who are smart enough to read this important book and share it with friends, the rewards will be there for years to come. Bravo, Patricia, for giving us all something nourishing to travel with on our life's journey."

—George C. Fraser, author of *Success Runs in Our Race*

"A wonderful book for youth and adults on living a good life from A to Z. An inspiring tool with many helpful nuggets for making it through the journey of life."

—Reatha Clark King, Ph.D., president and
executive director, General Mills Foundation

"In this book, Pat continues to inspire people through her motivational wisdom and creativity. This is a must-read for personal business and good fortune."

—Pat Harris, assistant vice president,
Diversity Initiatives, the McDonald's Corporation

"The content of Patricia Russell-McCloud's motivational book *A Is for Attitude* is wonderfully written as well as very powerful, inspirational, and upbeat. Not only does this book encourage readers to learn and grow internally, but it also helps the reader to apply simple concepts to [his or her] everyday life. Patricia provides valuable insight on issues that concern every one of us in some way or another. After reading this book, you will walk away with a renewed sense of self-worth, realizing your full potential. Everyone should have a copy of this book in his or her personal library."

—Valerie Daniels-Carter, president, Minority Franchise Owners Association, the Burger King Corporation

"Speaks to young and old, offering hope for tomorrow and fortitude and direction today."

—Felicia Hall, Women's Sports Marketing, Nike, Inc.

Dorsey Photography

About the Author

PATRICIA RUSSELL-MCCLOUD, a top-ranked motivational speaker who has spent more than fifteen years on the lecture circuit, has worked with General Motors, the Coca-Cola Company, Burger King, Bell South, and McDonald's, among others. For four years in a row, *Ebony* magazine named her one of the most influential people in the United States. A graduate of Kentucky State University and Howard University School of Law, she lives in Atlanta.

An
Alphabet
for
Living

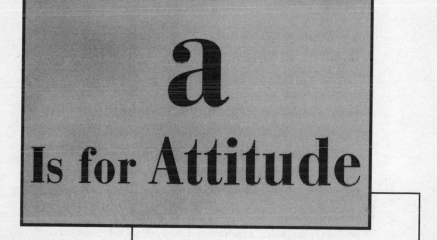

a
Is for Attitude

Patricia Russell-McCloud

Quill

An Imprint of HarperCollins*Publishers*

In dedication to my beloved mother

HarperCollins books may be purchased for educational, business, or sales promotional use. For information please write: Special Markets Department, HarperCollins Publishers Inc., 10 East 53rd Street, New York, NY 10022.

First Quill edition published 2002.

Designed by Christine Weathersbee

Library of Congress Cataloging-in-Publication Data is available.

ISBN 0-06-093233-3

02 03 04 05 06 FG/RRD 10 9 8 7 6 5 4 3

CONTENTS

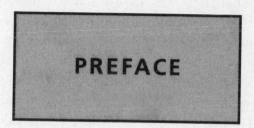

PREFACE

For the past several years, I have shared my version of the alphabet with audiences around the country. In my alphabet, each letter stands for an attribute or quality that can lead us to a better life. For example: A is for attitude, which determines your altitude, how high you will fly in this life; while C is for the courage to face all that life offers; and M is for meditation, and taking time to get to know yourself. Each time I recited these letters and the rest of this new alphabet for living, many people would approach me and request a copy of it. They said that they heard in this alphabet rich touchstones to change that they didn't want to soon forget. That is what has prompted me to write this book.

As for every speech I write, the inspiration for the original alphabet came from the wisdom and insight of my friends, family, mentors, protégés, heroes, and heroines. It also came from observing our experience; our individual trials, tribulations, and triumphs; and those qualities that always enabled us to get through the day and carry it forward—frequently with smiles on our faces and in our hearts. My goal was to touch the listener with this message: You are capable of far more than you believe. Rise up, believe in yourself and all the world offers, and take your place in the sun.

Writing *A is for Attitude: An Alphabet for Living* has given me the welcome opportunity to share all my thoughts on each letter of the alphabet and to convey to you more than a snippet of what each letter truly means to me. I found this experience fulfilling and cathartic. As I worked my way through each chapter, I discovered myself anew while remembering and facing the high moments and rough places of the human truths of who we are and how we are and what we can join together to do with and for one another. And each day, as I live, learn, and keep my finger on the pulse of now, the meaning of the alphabet becomes still richer.

Each chapter can become a new commitment for all of us to assess our strengths and fulfill more of our potential as individuals and as members of a global community. You might find that some of the chapters contain valuable lessons that can be applied over your lifetime.

Still others might give you insight into what's been standing in your way. Finally, some will have insights that actually move you to your next destination. Each letter is united by the common goal of calling on your need to be vigilant in your pursuit of the possible: To do less is to stifle your own potential.

It is my sincere hope that you will find in my book answers to pressing questions, a response to a deep yearning, some keys to a meaningful difference in your life, your family, and your community. And it is my heartfelt intent that by sharing a broad scope of inspiration, motivation, encouragement, truth, and personal experiences, I will connect with your head and heart. May your life be rich and full always. Rejoice!

a

Is for Attitude:
An Alphabet for Living

a

IS FOR ATTITUDE

Attitude Determines Your Altitude, How High You Will Fly in This Life

Your attitude is one of your greatest assets. It is your attitude and your thoughts that will determine whether you master all that is available to you from life's rich platter. Personally, I found that as long as I was afraid that a new challenge would be too much for me to handle, I was outmatched. For so long as I figured that my boss would find my suggestions wrong-headed, I was rejected. When I thought that I knew more than my companions, I didn't learn. And, finally, as long as I thought that I couldn't make a difference, I didn't make a difference. Once I made the decision that not much would change unless I first changed my mind, I was able to move forward. Only when I stood up, spoke up, opened up, and reached out was I able to move forward and take my place in the world. It was then that I discovered this powerful secret: Winners have a winning attitude.

Your thoughts direct what is and what will be, where you'll go and what you'll accomplish in your life. You alone determine how far you can go in life, and the possibilities are endless. No family members, friends, foes, teachers, counselors, mentors, preachers, or employers, no one else can determine your plight or progress. YOU can exceed your potential. YOU can exceed every test, every evaluation, every expectation, every study, every database, every demographic compilation of statistical information on like individuals who, by all reports, based on scientific analysis, should not go beyond where they are. You can do it! If you believe! In sum, your attitude determines your stretch!

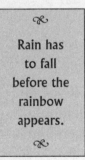

Rain has to fall before the rainbow appears.

Attitude can truly make you a winner. You can have an attitude that is optimistic, not eternally, but one that typically expects a brighter outcome. You always strive to work things out and you believe that nothing is beyond repair. Your heightened sense of personal power over and involvement with life events, coupled with a never-say-never posture, will serve you well in relationships and situations. This is especially true if you acknowledge the inevitability of hardships—rather than deny them—and allow people to help you face them. Keep the thought ever before you that rain has to fall before the rainbow appears.

In advocating a spirit of healthy self-confidence, I am not suggesting that you adopt a cocky attitude. Actually, if you choose arrogance—if you move from the premise that you know it all—then you close yourself off from the opportunity to learn from other people. Ironically, the more you think you know, the less you will know. Another limiting attitude is that of the eternal critic. If you decide to have a critical attitude, then every person or situation has to enter a narrow glass house for which you are the sole architect and builder and which you alone hold the floor plan. Such a judgmental nature shuts out a lot of people and blessings that don't meet your immediate specifications but that might enrich your life in the long run.

And let's not forget the eternal procrastinator. This attitude convinces you that life will be good and ready when you are good and ready. In reality, though, life is not a dress rehearsal; there are precious few do-overs or replays. Second chances are given to those who will really take the chances. Meanwhile, the procrastinator, the anytime-will-do person, never does get it done. Life does not wait for anyone.

Life does reward those who fully accept it on its own terms. With this attitude, you don't waste time grumbling about the hand you've been dealt; rather, you look at the cards and make the best possible play. It's a make-lemonade-with-lemons acceptance of life and it's guaranteed to propel you to the realization of your highest potential. Your refusal to throw a pity party for yourself in response to a reversal in fortune, your strong and silent strength of character, will attract many admirers to your side. You can cultivate this attitude by mediating on the wisdom of this adage: "I complained because I had no shoes, until I met a man who had no feet."

Just consider the experience of Pat McCormick, the first and only woman in Olympic history to win four gold medals in diving. The first time she tried out for the Olympic diving team in 1948, she just missed qualifying. Well, rather than give up and move on, Pat decided that she was not going to suffer that disappointment again. She trained even harder for the next Olympic tryouts, doing a hundred dives a day, six days a week. The next time, she not only qualified for the U.S. team, she also went on to sweep both diving golds in the 1952 and 1956 Olympics; the latter a remarkable eight months after the birth of her first child! Pat's attitude is one that we can all use to win gold: "The most important thing I know—when you have a dream and you really believe, YOU WILL FIND A WAY."

How can you get started in the right direction? Your first assignment is to stop whining. Stop the excuses and explanations and the rehearsal of the litany of self-imposed inhibitors that keep you forever in the attitude that you cannot go beyond where you are. Remember: "There are no victims, only volunteers." Every time you decide that the forces are working against you, your assets are being placed in a box with a lid and a lock. You alone hold the key. YOU have to be the one to discover your own treasures.

Your next assignment is to pay attention to everything that comes out of your mouth. Think carefully about what you say, how you say it, and to whom you say it. Above all, carry conversations forward in a positive, constructive, and meaningful way. Mastery in communication is vital. The Greek proverb states: "Act quickly: Think slowly." If you take the time to articulate your points clearly, concisely, and sincerely, matters of contention will tend to disappear or dissipate, for the true language of the

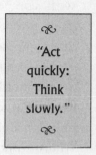

heart disarms opponents. Then remember to honor your words—whether spoken or written—for people want you to be as good as your pledge, as true as your promise, and as good as your word.

Have you ever had the experience of hearing one of your comments repeated to you a few days later and thinking in astonishment: "I said that?" If so, you might want to think about whether you're committed to speaking from your heart or whether your conversation is on remote control. Do you attach significance to the words you utter or do you just use them to fill dead space? In any case, please realize that others will assume that you really mean what you say and will act from that understanding. Make sure that your words reflect your truest feeling, belief, and attitude.

Your third and final assignment is to become aware of a different kind of communication: the messages you are sending with your body language. This unspoken language must align with the message you wish to transmit.

When you are in conversation with others, for instance, make sure that you give them your full attention. Look them in the eye and make sure that your eyes are in sync with your words. Also keep your body turned toward them and your arms relaxed at your sides (crossing your arms can send a message of defensiveness and closed-mindedness). If you are meeting with them in your office, look up from your pile of papers and let voice mail take your calls. Don't pick up the telephone, engage in a call, and then return to the conservation with "Now where were we?" That sends a message of arrogance and self-centeredness. If you are not interested in conversing with someone or if your interest is lukewarm, don't participate in the conversation. It is far kinder to beg out of a discussion than to engage in a distracted or disinterested way.

Even outside of conversation, you have to be mindful of your body language. Remember that the wrong look may be interpreted as a glare of hostility, a flip of the head can signal disinterest, a tap of the foot impatience. A turned back is dismissive and rude. Twisting a strand of hair communicates boredom or a coy come-on. A stooped posture conveys shame, fear, and low self-esteem. A posture of anger or any other negative response can be a telling barometer to others of your ability to practice maturity and self-control. Strategically, you must control your body language; otherwise, without a word, every unspoken thought, doubt, and judgment is readily expressed.

Have you ever seen someone completely control a situation without a word? It was probably a testament to the power of body language to send a message loud and clear. I'll never forget the way my mother had with this stern glare of hers. If any of us ever acted in a way that was inappropriate to the situation, she would shoot us a cold, uninterrupted stare. Without words and within seconds, her mere look brought us into line. It was direct, brought closure and consequence if ignored.

In addition to becoming more aware of the attitude expressed in your verbal and nonverbal communication, be meticulous in the choice of people with whom you surround yourself: They too send an important message about your values and intentions. And they can influence, reinforce, and even control your thinking. After you leave your friends' company, do you find your spirits consistently lifted, do you feel poised to be your best possible self? Or do you feel negative and pessimistic about other people and life in general? If your constant companions are narrow in their interests, judgmental, lacking purpose, creativity, imagination, and initiative, move on before you become stymied. Even worse, if it's clear that your "friends" are fair-weather and do not have your best interests at heart, don't linger a moment longer in their presence.

The game of life is worth one hundred plus points. Having the right people on your team will help you capture the most points. But, ultimately, it is your game, not only to play, but to conquer. Do not become detoured by others who offer dark opinions, give negative energy, or do not support your vision for your life. Instead, travel light, leave the naysayers behind, sitting on the sidelines.

If right now, you feel life is hard, maybe that's because you need to try harder. Look at yourself in the mirror, look deeply into your eyes until you see the limitless potential reflected therein. Your god knows that the person you see before you is capable of far more than you may ever realize. As you gaze at your reflection in the mirror, make a commitment to yourself to set a higher standard henceforth and raise the bar of personal excellence for yourself. You can accomplish all that and much more.

Here is an exercise that some people use to adjust their attitude and keep it elevated:

- Take a personal journal and make a list of your top ten personal assets (such as intelligence, loyalty, persistence and the like).

- Then make a list of your top ten personal defects (such as procrastination, negativity, poor organization).

- Make a list of the top ten goals you'd like to accomplish over the next twelve months.

- Reviewing your list of assets and defects, assess which ones support you and which ones get in your way as you work towards your goals.

- Each week for the next ten weeks, make a commitment to become more mindful of a particular pair of traits: one asset you want to nurture and a defect you'd like to diminish. Over the course of the week, (1) express gratitude for your asset and think about how it can help you reach your goals that day, and (2) find opportunities to work on lessening the hold of your defect (e.g., if the defect is impulsiveness, make a commitment to bring each work project to closure before diving into the next one).

- Imagine how your life will change and unfold as each of your ten goals comes true. Make a list about what you anticipate and keep it close at hand. When the going gets rough, pull it out and use it to remind you of the benefits of staying the course.

As you begin moving along this straight and steady path toward the accomplishment of your goals and dreams, you will discover that you alone set the pace and the place of your victory lap.

Remember that the hardest "A" grade ever achieved may be in the area in which you are most proficient. In my case, it was speech and drama. Despite my innate special talents in these areas, and maybe because of them, my teacher pushed me, insisting that good would not be good enough. Why should it be, when there was a best to be discovered within me! I'd expect nothing less from you.

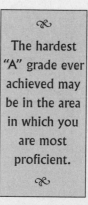

The hardest "A" grade ever achieved may be in the area in which you are most proficient.

Step forward with the discipline, determination, and knowledge that attitude determines your altitude, how high you will fly in this life. Strive, without stepping on anyone else in the process. Overcome obstacles, without being a walk-

ing advertisement of your self-assessed personal great-
ness. Set the mark and reach for it. The entire journey in
growth and self-development, whether quantum or
small, depends on you, alone.

Attitude is beyond mindset, for it encompasses your
thoughts and your actions. It determines how you
respond to your environment, and why you say and do
the things you do. It is an indication of your sensitivity
on an issue or your blatant disregard. Simply put, attitude is your choice.

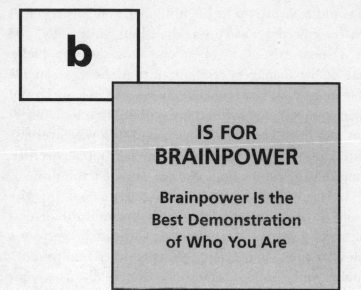

b

IS FOR BRAINPOWER

**Brainpower Is the
Best Demonstration
of Who You Are**

He's no rocket scientist." How many times have you heard that dismissive comment? Well, the funny thing about it is, as often as this comment's made, it doesn't get any smarter. "He" doesn't need to be a rocket scientist, nor do you. "He" does need to make the most of the mind he's been given, and so do you and so can you.

A friend of mine grew up as the daughter of a rocket scientist, believe it or not. Her father was one of the NASA scientists who worked out the equations for the first successful lunar landing. She always felt awed and intimidated by her father's intelligence; she never felt she could measure up to his brilliance and so she didn't even try. She did so-so in school, took so-so jobs, and had a so-so existence. Then one day, she was lucky: Some of her managers recognized that she was capable of far more than she realized, challenged her to step up to her potential, and offered her a promotion to management. At first, she resisted, saying, "It's way over my head!" But her boss would have none of that, answering, "Jump in, the water's fine, and we won't let you drown." So she took on the job, succeeded in boosting the morale of her team and leading them toward their first profitable year. As her success surpassed everyone's wildest dreams, her rocket scientist father said proudly, "Finally you're doing something that really uses your brain." The real benefit wasn't more money or a more challenging position, but that finally my friend knew she had a brain to use.

If you've been majoring in the minor, sitting on the sidelines of life, thinking that you must have been hiding when God handed out brains, think again. Only this time, think: "I am capable of doing anything if I put my mind to it." Then get up and use your head and watch your brainpower rocket you to new heights.

Consider the wisdom of that popular aphorism "As a man thinketh in his heart so is he." In his book *As a Man Thinketh*, James Allen meditated on that, saying:

A man's mind may be likened to a garden, which may be intelligently cultivated or allowed to run wild; but whether cultivated or neglected, it must and will, bring forth. If no useful seeds are put into it, then an abundance of useless weed-seeds will fall therein, and will continue to produce their kind.

Your intellectual development depends largely on how you use your mind. If you opt for laziness, abdicate best choices or crisp approaches to others, exert no effort to manifest your will, you will be sidelined. "Kicked to the curb." You will be subordinate, not primary; a footnote, an add-on, and parenthetical to those who have made the decision to invest in their brainpower.

Your brain is a complex and sensitive instrument, finely wired with divine circuitry that enables you to find and express meaning, deal with pleasure and pain, calmly cope with both emergencies or the routine, and fully sense all that surrounds you. Like all instruments, it needs regular tuning to stay in shape. Challenging yourself to create fresh approaches to old problems, to explore unfamiliar places, to debate and dissect received truths, to spend time with people whose wisdom forces you to stretch, to grapple with complex information—all these activities will help you to develop your intellectual property. And that property is one of the most precious gifts you possess and share—especially on the job.

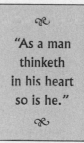

"As a man
thinketh
in his heart
so is he."

Sadly, many young people are not seizing every

opportunity to develop their minds before entering the work world. The *New York Times* recently reported that fewer and fewer young men are opting for college. Some enter the workplace and are underemployed; too many have joined the ranks of the uninspired unemployed, and others have found themselves resorting to the vices of the street. Certainly all of them are suffering through lives of unfulfilled potential. We are all the poorer for their unrealized potential.

My fear is that many young men mistakenly believe that brawn can substitute for brain in the real world, that they can live by the sweat of their brow alone. They're dead wrong. Ask any elite athlete and he'll tell you: Brainpower undergirds brawn power. The athlete needs to be able to think strategically so that he can leverage his prowess at shooting hoops, running the field or court, volleying the ball, or finishing the eighteenth hole of golf under par. Think about it: What makes Michael Jordan superior to other athletes? There are other players with his physical stature and musculature and willingness to train long hours, but they don't possess his most valuable characteristics: his drive, his will to win, and his uncanny genius for the game. In short, they do not have Michael Jordan's brainpower.

> ✑
>
> Your brain is a complex and sensitive instrument, finely wired with divine circuitry.
>
> ✑

Off the playing field too, successful business managers or owners will say they want to hire thinkers who can work fast and who can operate the new technology, which often demands a mind trained to work in more abstract and sophisticated ways than a high school education affords. And given the fast pace of the business environment, these businesses are hungry for workers who can take initiative and write their own directions.

Have you heard the latest buzzwords in the business world? When I speak to corporate audiences, I hear words such as *knowledge workers*, *knowledge management*, *cognitive competence*, and *knowledge-driven era*. Regardless of the industry, it seems that corporate management has arrived at the position that its true competitive advantage lies in harnessing the brainpower of its employees. Further, given the rapid speed of change in modern markets, the growth of global competition, and the greater amount of information and options available to us all, there's an increasing awareness that those people with fast, flexible minds are best poised to succeed in the twenty-first century.

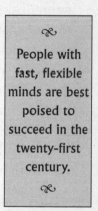

People with fast, flexible minds are best poised to succeed in the twenty-first century.

Does that frighten you? It need not. Wisdom abounds; it's yours for the taking. Life itself is full of academic courses. Learn the lessons. Any new undertaking—whether you're starting the first day in school or on a new job, or you're interacting with a different group of people for the first time, or you're visiting a new city or country—is rich with the opportunity to gain new insight, self-knowledge, and worldly intelligence. To partake, you must bring your full attention to the experience, suspend prejudgment, and listen with the intention to learn. Some clues that you're not present to the situation, that you're operating on automatic pilot: You take the yellow slip when the blue one is called for; you find yourself on corridor A, not B; you're consulting the wrong briefing book; you can't distinguish one day from the next; or you find it hard to be a part of the conversation. If that's been going on in your life, don't be hard on yourself. Maybe you needed to plateau for a period. Just don't stay there. Make the decision to grab hold of the master controls and move forward with your life.

Whatever your chosen endeavor—leader or follower— you'll need the intellectual ability to address the salient issues that present themselves each day. If you determine that you are going to be equipped to handle whatever comes your way, you must always strive to cultivate your brainpower so that your mind can become a catalytic force for positive change not only in your life but also in the lives of those who touch yours. The brain is the most powerful change agent we have.

A case in point is forensic psychiatrist and friend, Rosalind E. Griffin, M.D., the first in her family to go to college and graduate. Dr. Griffin added the optional study of sign language to her arsenal of required coursework so that she would be prepared to work with persons who were deaf if they needed her services. She felt a calling to reach out to this population, which so often feels invisible and isolated—particularly once she found out that only sixty American psychiatrists (only one of whom resided in her home state of Michigan) were fluent in American Sign Language. Her actions demonstrate her fervent belief in the adage: "To those whom much is given, much is required." Today, as the medical director of Deaf Counseling Services Center at Detroit Medical Center, she assists in navigating deaf people to a safe harbor in mental health treatment. In making the choice during her medical training to use her brainpower to the fullest and learn ASL, Dr. Griffin has gone on to provide the deaf the same entitlement that all citizens are granted in eliminating barriers to their productivity.

Keep learning. Pursue more training, degrees, adventures, and travel: Each in its own way stretches your mind and helps you to keep your brainpower well-fueled. For instance, when you travel, you have the opportunity to embrace the world's offerings, to meet new people and learn their culture, to discover special customs and traditions, and even to find new tried-and-true ways to handle your own everyday affairs. Then too, when you are thrust into an unfamiliar situation, you are often forced to become more resourceful, to think in new ways, and to move outside your comfort zone: As you travel through large cities and small villages and see bright lights and barren back roads, your horizons are being continually widened and you return to your own life recharged, refreshed, and infused with new wisdom and perspective.

Formal education is another way that you can expose yourself to new and different information, outside of what has become your established routine of experience. I opted for advanced education and took the time to get a law degree. After graduation, I practiced law for ten years, and I was very proud to be a member of the profession. At some point, though, I felt my old calling as an orator reawaken, and I knew that the few speeches I had time to give in and around my law career were not going to be enough to satisfy this desire. So, fifteen years ago, I dedicated myself to a new full-time career as a professional orator and I have never looked back. Does that mean that I regret all the time and money and effort invested in pursuing a legal career? Not a bit. I remain proud of the work I accomplished as a lawyer for the Federal Communications Commission, and I cherish the relationships I made in my years in Washington. And my law school education and experience as a regulatory lawyer taught me new analytical tools and gave me the courage to advocate passionately for justice; both these gifts continue to enrich my personal and professional life.

As each new learning experience opens up new vistas to you, take time to evaluate your old ideas. You'll find that many are worthy and stand the test of time. Wherever you find yourself, remain planted firmly in your core values and belief system. If you've subscribed to age-old maxims like "Begin with the end in mind," "What goes around comes around," and "If you make your bed hard, that's where you're going to lie," you'll probably find that they can coexist comfortably with the new insights you've gained. Other beliefs may have fit at one point but no longer make sense and need adjustment. For example, you might have believed that you could handle everything on your own; as you grow and mature and become aware of our increasingly interdependent world, however, you perhaps have begun to realize that there is more strength in community than in self-sufficiency. Or you might have held views that were toxic: Perhaps you presumed that highly attractive people never had to work hard and actually aren't very intelligent. Such a jealous view clearly is irrational, unjust, and unproductive—and can contaminate a more sage perspective. Cast such views aside immediately and make room for better ideas to take root.

As you make room for new ideas, question old truths, and flex your brain muscle, be prepared: You'll find the boat will rock before it moves forward. Thinking can be disturbing and unsettling, and can cause restlessness on both sides of the aisle. Some will become angry, because you offer the unconventional agenda, have a difference of opinion, raise questions that should have been asked and answered long ago. Others will become vexed, "threatened" by the fact that you have the intelligence and commit-

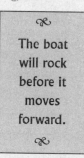

The boat will rock before it moves forward.

ment to fix what is broken. As you rock the boat, upset the old apple cart, and detour from the way things have always been done, you probably won't find yourself surrounded by cheerleaders.

You will need to develop new allies. For there will be those who stubbornly resist change at all costs and who either are captured by yesterday or belong to a different era altogether. Don't ignore your detractors completely, though. Instead, build on their knowledge, whether it's in the professional, personal, or institutional arenas.

On the home front, if you're someone who has been shy or passive in most of your relationships, always on "standby" waiting for the other person to decide what is best, your new confidence in your ability to think for yourself is going to cause a very dramatic shift in all your relationships. Don't let that deter or frighten you. You've hidden your light behind the bushel for long enough. It's time that the world had a chance to see all the unique intelligence you possess. From now on, you hold the carte blanche; you no longer need anyone else's permission in handling the affairs or circumstances of your life. It's yours to live. From now on, if you don't care for the taste of all the ingredients cooked in someone else's pot, prepare your own.

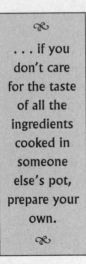

... if you don't care for the taste of all the ingredients cooked in someone else's pot, prepare your own.

Leaders have a desire to learn and cultivate a curiosity for new dimensions of knowledge, becoming life-long learners with a perpetual sense of wonder. They strive for wisdom and do not confuse it with wit. Leaders thrive on integrity, recognizing that without integrity all other ingredients of leadership will not matter.

Society actually wants and needs you to take charge of your own life. There's a universal craving for thinkers in a time when, for example, too many of the nation's children have learned to multiply before they have learned to subtract. Use your brain to be a positive agent for change. And, as you meet some inevitable resistance from some fellow travelers, remember that anonymous members of society do not exist. Each of us has an obligation to pay for the space we occupy and no privileges are afforded for noninvolvement. Engage!

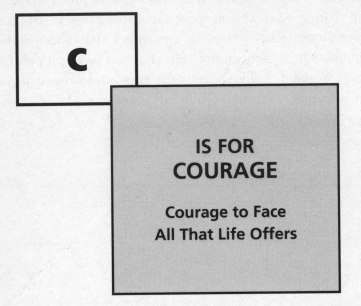

C

IS FOR COURAGE

Courage to Face All That Life Offers

Life is not for sissies. Most of what is worthwhile, meaningful, and real lies on the other side of your comfort zone. If you've been spending a lot of time in your comfort zone—if you've got it all arranged and decorated just so—your life is probably in a rut. You owe it to yourself and those who love and depend on you to break out and try something different. That action will take courage, chutzpah, guts, or sheer will. The choice of words is your own and so is the choice of action.

Try something different. Hold your forefinger and thumb an inch apart. It's just a small space, but it's substantial if you will fill it with something new and different. In your life, do something with just that much difference as a first step in breaking your routine. For instance, if you're afraid of social situations, when you're at your next gathering, make a decision to meet three new people and to discover three facts about their lives. Or, if you're timid about speaking up at business meetings, make the commitment to share one piece of pertinent information at each meeting. Then again, if you're scared to try out new things or places, once a week, plan a field trip and sample a new restaurant or visit a different museum.

All the little voluntary changes you make, however inconsequential they may seem, are very significant. Each is an opportunity to face and overcome fear and to deepen your courage. These everyday experiences prepare you to handle those surprise situations that demand a huge leap of faith and a deep reservoir of courage. In daily nutritional needs, experts have clearly described the benefits of fiber being a part of a balanced daily diet. You need fiber as a part of your daily temperament, too!

During my good old college days I pledged a sorority, alone. Usually there's a "pledge class," a group of freshman or sophomore students who all hope to join the same sorority and who pledge together over a certain period of time. Depending on the sorority, the sisters will test the pledges' merit (and mettle) with prescribed community or campus activities. I found myself working around the clock to complete the required academic review sessions; keep the prescribed hours at the library; carry out the various clean-up, fix-up, or paint-up community campaigns; and prepare my performance for the all-Greek Pan-Hellenic show for the entire student body. Usually, there's a pledge class of wannabes who support one another through the grueling pledge period. That year, though, I was the only woman who pledged the Alpha Kappa Alpha Sorority, Inc., and I had to go it alone.

At the time, I was only nineteen years old and I was pretty shy. Being the only pledge for my sorority and having to serenade all the other students as they filed into the cafeteria at mealtime, standing up alone at pep rallies to perform our cheer, and performing the other solo pledge activities called a lot of unwanted attention to me. But as embarrassed as I was, being a member of that sorority and getting involved in community works meant more to me than any passing humiliation. I kept my attention focused on the end game and on the people who recognized and applauded my tenacity in pledging alone and tuned out those who made fun of my situation. Also I remembered Shakespeare's classic words "A coward dies many times before his death" and I added to it the modern motto: "Never say die."

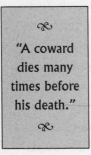

"A coward dies many times before his death."

I got through and it made me a better person. Every day of the pledging process, I discovered a new dimension of myself. Every day I learned fortitude, perseverance, determination, and commitment, but, most of all, I learned courage. It doesn't seem like a big deal to me now, but at the time, it took me way, way out of my comfort zone. It stretched me. And it prepared me for later experiences like signing the contract for my new job as a first-year teacher for the Detroit Public Schools, moving to a city where I knew only my uncle. I did not have a car and I did not know how to drive. Although I was terrified, I stood straight and moved on.

Visualize big puffy clouds, all beautiful and filled with air. Our words and deeds can seem just as pretty and vacuous when we lack sincerity and deep sensitivity to what really counts in life. Think about it. More often than not, do you "say what you mean and mean what you say"? Are you courageous enough to say yes to going against the grain, rattling the cage, rocking the boat, stepping away from the voices of the masses and letting your voice be heard as you cast a vote for that which is alien but appropriate?

Let's put it another way: Would you rather be the leader or the led? True leaders don't check the polls before taking action. Despite a deafening stream of individual complaints, queries, and resistance, they remain committed to a collective good and try to shape the consensus to that vision. Take the lead for those who are worthy of your dedicated commitment; identify the community need, communicate openly through your words and deeds, and then refuse to be deterred. Make very certain that your mind, body, and spirit are in alignment with your outer resolve. Take strength from the possibility that it's part of the divine plan that you swim forth, against the tide, with fresh, vibrant, sparkling ideas while others may well be drowning in the shallow end.

Decide. There is a separation between right and wrong and action and inaction. Move beyond tenuous and ambivalent thinking. Everybody has an opinion. So press on. Prepare for unpopularity when being true to yourself requires the drawing of a figurative line in the sand and taking an unalterable position. Stand firm. Stand tall.

Imagine yourself as the chief on-site engineer, who is asked to build success. You wouldn't start the project by selecting the caterer for the banquet occasion honoring its triumphant conclusion. Instead, you would think like an engineer and start with the foundation. You would want to make sure that the base could withstand everything that man, weather, and acts of God might deliver. Kudos, plaques, awards, and expressions for a job well done may be offered upon completion of the structure. The first step, however, is to lay down a foundation that is sure. In the case of your success, it will stand or fall on the strength of your courage and conviction. That's your base.

It takes courage to keep commitments that make a difference, for in making a difference, you are creating a change, and change often frightens many who may try to oppose you at all costs. Meanwhile, those you are taking the time to help might not acknowledge, much less reward, your "generosity" with undying gratitude. Let me give you a quick example. In Atlanta, I participated in an Adopt-a-School program, wherein I helped to mentor and provide companionship for middle-school students. Once a month, I, along with other volunteers, took the time to painstakingly prepare informative and entertaining workshops that would introduce the children to lifelong learning skills, ranging from academic habits to matters of social etiquette. At first, some of the kids acted out, showed off for each other through rebellious behavior, and tested the limits of all of us volunteers. With fortitude, I remained with others who, courageous in spirit, stuck with the program and kept showing up month after month despite the kids' ungrateful behavior. We learned that the students had been disappointed by some previous Adopt-a-School volunteers, who'd provided spotty programming and shown up inconsistently. It took time and courage for my group to stick it out and win the kids' trust. You see, when you are working with people of any age, notwithstanding your credentials, the maxim is correct: "People want to know that you care, before they care what you know." It takes an abundant amount of courage to care and to show that you really care.

> ❧
> Swim forth, against the tide, with fresh, vibrant, sparkling ideas while others may well be drowning in the shallow end.
> ❧

It takes courage to interact with other people in an authentic way—whether those people are middle-school students or next-door neighbors. It takes real courage to be "up close and personal" with those who are, at first glance, different—particularly if you're naturally shy like me. One thing that helped me to overcome my self-consciousness was to think more about other people. I realized that I really wasn't that different. All people seek some level of acceptance and belonging. All people have fears and failings. All people have a need to forgive and to be forgiven. The issue is simply whether, when, and how we will seek to respond individually or collectively to our mutual needs.

Several months ago, a group of anxious members of my church, a predominantly black congregation, joined with a white congregation to pursue an ecumenical effort to address racism through anti-racism training. The program moved from the premise that racism related to power. Wow! It was a courageous step for both sides to agree to sit down once a month with people who, in many ways, seemed different, and to try to understand differing perspectives while truthfully seeking to evaluate our own. We had some brutally honest exchanges in plain black and white, and not in shades of gray, wherein we found that each side really did not know what the other one was talking about or going through. It was very tense at moments and it took a lot of courage to participate, but we were rewarded with healing and transformation. Black participants were shocked to witness whites' naïveté about the many real instances of racism that most blacks endure on a daily basis. Whites, meanwhile, were surprised to learn that blacks assumed that their ignorance signaled indifference or, worse yet, complicity with racist attitudes and actions.

Blacks were disappointed to hear one white professional say that his small engineering firm could not attract "qualified blacks" for they would surely work for larger firms to gain more opportunities. Blacks concluded, without variation, that this statement was an often used and rarely substantiated excuse to not hire blacks. Whites were shocked to hear of real estate agents routinely asking black homeowners to hide all ethnically oriented art, coffee table books, and magazines when their homes were being shown to potential buyers. All agreed that it was interesting their taste in a home was good enough to display, but neither their culture nor appreciation in art could pass a buyer's viewing test. (Please!) All of us began to see the world more through the others' eyes and feel a stronger shared bond.

Personally, I learned through these sessions, sometimes painfully, the degree to which I had become increasing guarded and a bit cynical when it came to cross-cultural human relations. I realized that I rarely accepted white people's intentions at face value; rather I tended to analyze, second-guess, probe for a subagenda. Even though intellectually I fervently believed in the power and possibility of multiculturalism to uplift all involved, old wounds made it hard for me to trust and always act according to that rational understanding. This program helped me to see that I had to have the courage to lay down my automatic defenses and to risk trusting white people to walk the talk, unless proven otherwise.

All of life's trials are not manmade. The time will come to us all when the spirit is willing, but the body is weak. A wonderful friend, who has been a powerful role model and stalwart for her many admirers, encountered three monumental life challenges in quick succession. First, she lost her beloved husband (after their golden wedding anniversary), then her nationally known, physically fit son died suddenly, and, finally, she was diagnosed with cancer.

In small and large ways, this woman had always lived life on life's terms; she never tried to adjust it to fit herself or to deny reality. Her character served her well in her sickness. At every stage of the disease, when her numerous friends asked about her well-being, she simply responded, "I am doing just fine." She never complained or asked, "Why me?" She accepted her disease and expressed gratitude for all that life had given her. Even after chemotherapy, when nearly all her hair had fallen out, this beautiful spirit worried more about our discomfort than her own. She jokingly reassured us that she'd decided to try a new hairstyle.

The treatments and her positive attitude helped her to withstand the cancer for a while. Ultimately, though, the disease marched through her body and won the war. In the final days, she wondered aloud why so many people were fretting over her. She had no fear. She had always lived each day as though it were her last. Living as if there were no tomorrow and meeting life's ultimate conclusion with dignity and grace: This is the ultimate demonstration of courage in action. Take heart!

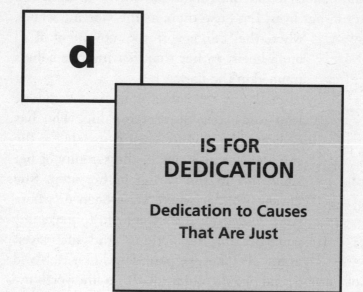

d

IS FOR
DEDICATION

**Dedication to Causes
That Are Just**

Each of us is a sleek and powerful car hugging the curves of life. Like that car, our wheels are vital, they keep us rolling along the highway. Unlike a car's, though, our wheels aren't made out of rubber and steel. Our right front wheel is family, our left front wheel is education, the back left wheel represents economics, and the right back wheel represents our social network. In the trunk, the spare tire represents our personal values or our "calling" card. There is only one thing wrong with this scenario. The qualities of devotion stashed in the trunk should be more centrally located. Rather than hiding our beliefs, let us think about putting them front and center in our lives. Let's use them as the steering wheel, where they can govern the movement of all our wheels, rather than leaving our beliefs trapped in the dark.

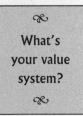

She doesn't wonder where she's been or where she's going, nor does she need to make any apologies for her actions.

You can tell when you meet someone who leads a value-centered life, who has dedicated her life to a just cause. It's in the shine of her eyes, it's in the serenity of her smile, it's in the spring in her step. She doesn't wonder where she's been or where she's going, nor does she need to make any apologies for her actions. And she never, ever feels lonely or poor. Her life is rich and full of purpose and people and pride. It's a life worth living and sharing.

Do you know what you value most? Many years ago, someone asked me, "What's your value system?" I thought, "Value system? What's that supposed to mean?" When I responded with a blank look, he suggested, "Look at your checkbook, look at your agenda. Wherever your time and money live, that's where your treasure lies." That was a wake-up call. There in black and white, spelled out before me, I saw very clearly where I was investing myself, and it didn't square with what my heart and soul treasured. Actually, I felt ashamed. But with that shame came awareness and the opportunity to do things differently.

What's your value system?

Right now, I invite you to get your checkbook and

your planner and take a look at those people, places, and things to which you have been dedicating yourself. How do you feel about it? Do you want to make any shifts in your allotments? Are there any aspects of your life or the life of your community that have received scant attention? Are there others that have received more than their fair share? What can you do on a daily basis to bring these things into alignment?

What is most important to you? When I was young, that sort of question scared me, and it sometimes still does. My fear is that there's a right or wrong answer and I'll fail the test. In truth, there are as many right ways to answer that question as there are people in this world. If you feel scared when you hear that question and you find your mind going a little blank, here's a visualization exercise to help you start to get a handle on your true north, your authentic values. Close your eyes, take a deep breath, and get in a comfortable position. In your mind's eye, imagine yourself on one side of a raging, whitewater river with a thin, slippery log stretching across to the opposite bank. Visualize someone in jeopardy on the other side of the bank that gets you so frightened that you quickly cross the log to help. What did you see? Who or what propelled you to risk your own life for its sake? That's where your passion and dedication lie.

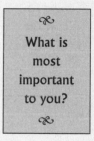

What is most important to you?

Here's another way to pinpoint your cause célèbre: Think about the last time you went beyond the call of duty for something or someone else. What drove you?

Were you trying to get "attaboys" on the back or to add another impressive stunt to your résumé? Or did it go deeper? Was it connected to a spiritual calling? Was it a mission that took on a life of its own?

If you haven't ever committed yourself to something beyond getting past the next nine to five, it's time that you got involved. There is too much to be done, and no one's talent can be spared. The worthy programs, projects, and activities are enough to consume every extra minute, hour, week, and month of our collective schedules. You don't need to do it all: You do need to do something. Social engagement is our personal prerogative and privilege in the next century.

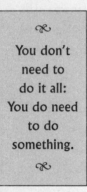

You don't need to do it all: You do need to do something.

Pull your ego over to the curb and park it. Put some coins in your mental meter while you take a walking trip to explore what you can do to lift the word *response* from the word *responsibility*, to make your life mission more than a laminated statement tucked in your wallet, to put action behind all those good intentions, to grab all the opportunity that lies before you to make a difference for others. It's time to get over yourself and out to the rest of the world. You're late for a command performance!

Decide that you are able to identify and respond to the problems, policies, and conditions that determine (or are inimical to) the quality of life. Become convinced that you have the ability to do what needs to be done and the willingness to use what you have to get what is wanted. From now on, you are an opportunity magnet, constantly taking the pulse of each new situation. You think for the long and short haul, not just for the moment, not just for yourself. If you indulge in focusing on the short term and if you use your own narrow self-interest as the only guide, then you yourself have become a part of the major source of the problems prevalent today.

Some of my sweetest and best memories come from my work for just causes. Moments that I've spent working for improvements in education and housing have written some of the finest chapters in my memory book and brought contentment to my heart. I once spent time in my hometown of Atlanta working on a Habitat for Humanity house. Habitat for Humanity is a hands-on charitable organization that provides financing and manpower (through volunteer joint ventures with corporations, clubs, or other nonprofits whose members are dedicated to helping the homeless) to help low-income families build their homes. The day we completed a house in Atlanta, I shared with the other volunteers the poignant gift of a mother's gratitude as she walked into her new home. She said, with tears in her eyes: "Even working two jobs, I would never have been able to buy a house, trying to take care of my two sons, my daughter, and my grandmother at the same time." Knowing I helped make a difference in that family's life was worth more than all the applause in the world to me. She touched my heart.

Your cause and mine might not match. You might not care deeply about housing or education. We each have our own rich history and culture that play a role in choosing those things that deserve our dedication. You might find that park preservation or helping handicapped children or dancing with the elderly or feeding the hungry or establishing car-free zones or another one of the millions of causes is more your speed. That's great. Our just causes vary and they are more numerous than blades of grass and they all need sympathizers to move from audience to army; to become a donor and to lend a hand. Pick the cause that you believe in and then do the work.

A friend of mine wasn't involved in service work and he was feeling guilty about it. Rick explained to me that at one time he worked weekly in a city soup kitchen housed in a dark, dank basement. They fed five hundred or more homeless men three times a week within a matter of hours. He was proud of what the kitchen accomplished and he felt good about playing a role, but he didn't enjoy going there and he gradually made excuses not to show up. When I pressed him about this paradox, he finally admitted (with great embarrassment) that he couldn't stand the stifling smell in the tight, poorly ventilated serving quarters. So rather than ask to switch jobs (perhaps helping to prepare the food), my friend felt ashamed of his discomfort and allowed it to push him away.

Life is not a game of entitlement. In life, we are all given certain gifts. Those who appreciate their gifts as such, and who freely pass them on, most often find their gestures rewarded ten-fold. If you approach life with an eye toward what you have and what you have to give others, you will lead a fuller life. The way of the open hand, the way of service, is an attitude that also leads to higher self-esteem. Think of those people who have blinked back tears and who have given support rather than seeking it, and how their attitude of selflessness and commitment to the well-being of others earned your respect and awe.

We are not saints! If you try your hand at some volunteer work and it's not your cup of tea, try something else. Another friend of mine, who had no sense of smell, relished her work in that very same soup kitchen where Rick worked. She made friends with the regular "customers" and loved joking around with them (and they with her) so much that it got her out of bed at four-thirty A.M. in order to lend a hand before starting her workday. Let me assure you, she's no martyr. It's her sense of fun (and smell) that is quite different from Rick's. "Different strokes" applies to dedication too!

Admittedly, there are times when we're inactive, when inertia has taken the controls. It is easy, too easy, to follow the crowd, and to affirm the lack of action by the masses. Very often it is easy to do nothing and avoid committing to something concrete, which takes you to a higher level of meaning and obligation in your life. That's an easy choice but an empty one. Go for the joy!

What can you do? No matter where you live, no matter how busy your schedule or what you have to work with, there's something you can do immediately to make a difference. You can defend a person who has been unfairly treated; you can speak in support of those falsely accused; you can share your resources with someone in need; you can hail a cab for the vision-impaired, and you can work to ensure victory when defeat seems imminent.

What else can you do? Take an inventory of your belongings. Check the closet in your dressing area, the chest of drawers, the extra closet in the guest bedroom, the under-the-bed storage, the trunks, the garage, and the kitchen cupboards. Ask yourself whether you really need all that you have. Then invite your friends to do the same thing and to convene at your house for a brunch and swap meet. There you can trade things you don't need for things that you do. (You also can trade laughs about the dubious taste that once led you to buy those cowboy boot–shaped rhinestone earrings or those orange denim bell-bottoms or the duck decoy sculpture!) At the end of the day, you can pack up a car or two with all the unclaimed "treasures" and drive them to a local charity.

When the brisk days of winter started, I was asked to donate my only trench coat to a clothes closet. My first thoughts focused on how many more times I could wear the coat and when and where it was purchased. Then I learned that the person for whom the coat had been requested had only a sweater. I thought of my advantage and, without hesitation, gave the coat away. Whether or not my coat brought a smile to her face, I do know that it brought warmth to my heart.

In my travels, I often hear from people who are brokenhearted and lonely. Love is the great cure, and you feel it when you give it with no strings attached. I've found in my own life that the fastest way to find a community of like-minded, loving, and lovable people is to search out a cause that speaks to my heart. That's where I'll find my family—new and old.

Medical advances have extended our life expectancy and swollen the elderly population, who are living longer, but not necessarily better. Even those with well-intentioned families feel lonely for new friends, outside companionship and interest. Ours is a culture that celebrates youth and discards the old. And yet age is more than a stage, passage, or number: It is a reality. It will catch you—all you have to do is keep living. You can share and prepare for it by giving some of your time and attention to helping elderly persons move toward a new level of self-sufficiency or even picking up the phone and placing a call so they know they still belong. Are you really that busy?

Life is surely more than mere existence. It is involvement beyond the confines of the sanctuary of our thoughts, concepts, and culture. Life is an extension of self to involve oneself in the enrichment of others. Simply, true satisfaction is found in giving; as they say, "It is its own reward." Within the best of us, there is a better. Witness this evidence of "better":

- Mother Teresa left the safety of the convent to work in the slums serving the poorest of the poor in Calcutta. At the time of her death, her name was whispered in churches and screamed in the streets throughout her country. Our assignment: that we not let our commemoration of her deeds outweigh our movement to the same.

- Cosmetic surgeon Brad Herman, M.D.,
travels the world providing pro bono plastic
surgeries to those disfigured by birth defects,
cleft palates, tumors, or burns. His mission,
dubbed Operation Smile, is to boost their
quality of life.

  A twelve-year-old Kenyan boy walked and
hitchhiked 150 miles to the designated site
for medical assistance, arriving after the clinic
closed. An attending physician found him, took
him in, corrected his cleft palate in forty-five
minutes, and changed his life forever.

- Neither royalty nor commoners expected
Lady Diana, Princess of Wales, to fight for the
removal of land mines or to touch those infected
by HIV/AIDS. Her celebrity and unapologetic
presence, awareness, and commitment to
unpopular causes raised the consciousness
of all who would dedicate themselves to
justice.

- The persistence of Dr. Martin Luther King, Jr.,
stalwart civil rights leader, drum major for justice, spoke the truth for equality for all people,
declaring, that "we must stand for something or
we will fall for anything."

These are the dedicated who have inspired and com-
manded our attention. Millions more give minutes,
hours, days, weeks, years in quiet and constant battle for

causes they believe in. There's room and
need for everyone to take a role.

Our personal encounters in life afford
great windows of chance to reach outside
ourselves to make a personalized, custom-
made contribution. Let there be a marriage
in your life between good intentions, and
personal engagement. Let the vow of "I do"
be yours.

> ❧
> "We must
> stand for
> something
> or we will
> fall for
> anything."
> ❧

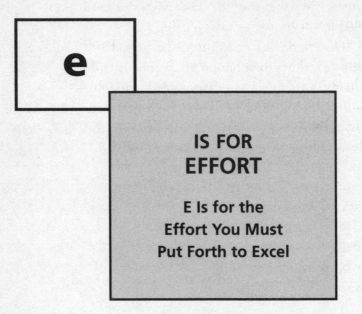

e

IS FOR EFFORT

E Is for the Effort You Must Put Forth to Excel

There is personal honor and glory in every moment that you give your best, regardless of the outcome. You might not receive a ribbon or a trophy or a standing ovation or any form of material recognition. Your reward lies elsewhere.

Even after giving your all, you must be prepared sometimes to receive a below-par evaluation; a rating of good, not best; a score of seven out of ten; and the role of support staff, not team leader. Meanwhile, someone else who apparently has hardly tried, who has applied half the effort you did, might win all the kudos. Adjust. It is called life.

Too often I've seen talented people put their heart and soul into a project and then give up at the first sign of failure. There was a novelist I met who spent eight long years working on a manuscript. As soon as he finished, he sent it out to two literary agents. Both rejected it, and he simply gave up. He took the manuscript and the eight years of effort behind it and he stuck it on a shelf, and he has never written another line. When he told me this story, I listened in silent frustration. I wanted to roll back time and coach him to send his manuscript out to more agents (there are hundreds, all with different tastes and preferences) and to start writing his next novel in the meantime. You see, he didn't lack talent or opportunity; he lacked effort. That's true for most of us, most of the time.

One day, a friend called me and asked as usual, "How's it going?" I was feeling low that day about work; it was one of those days when I felt that the more work I did, the more there was to do, and even my best effort was not enough. I told her "I'm having a hard time of it." She was a true friend,

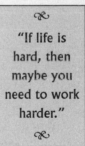

"If life is hard, then maybe you need to work harder."

so rather than respond with an "Oh, poor Pat!" she said to me, "If life is hard, then maybe you need to work harder." Honestly, it wasn't what I wanted to hear, but it was what I needed to hear. It got my rear in gear.

Assume that you are one of the 99.9 percent of people who have to work for what they get. In life, that is really the only safe assumption to make. Things don't just happen. Academic degrees and job promotions are earned, not determined by luck, wish, or intent, or simply given away. Yes, even those people who get ahead because they know the right people know the right people because they made the effort. Rather than begrudge the importance of networking, accept it and start making your own connections. As one person wisely said, "If you are going to be a squeaky wheel, you have to be around the one who has the grease."

> ᘏ
> Assume that you are one of the 99.9 percent of people who have to work for what they get.
> ᘏ

Personal initiative does count in the long run, and it will have a great deal to do with your success. For example, if "showing up is half the battle," then show up early and you'll get the advantage. Remember, "Nothing comes to a sleeper but a dream, and when he wakes up even the dream is gone!" So turn off the snooze button. Refuse to be the last one there or the first one to leave: The extra time invested demonstrates you are a serious contender.

Don't subscribe to the idea that I call the "lucky star theory." This is the belief that those who succeed were born under the right star or in the right place or to the right parents or at the right time. If you believe this, then you probably also believe that if you don't succeed, it doesn't mean that you didn't try hard enough, you just have bad luck. It's time to grow up!

Since I was a young child, I've been told that I'm a talented speaker, and I do acknowledge God for this gift. I also must acknowledge that I have nurtured, and continue to nurture, this gift on a daily basis. I didn't become a top-ranked speaker by opening my mouth one day. All peak performers, whether in the arts or business or athletics or law or medicine, work their craft. A dance group rehearses its choreography, actors and actresses rehearse their lines, lawyers undertake mock trials, and writers go through numerous rewrites. In all cases, the consistency of their practice, their consistent pursuit of excellence, is more essential to their success than their innate talent. It takes hard work to deliver an effortless performance.

Today, as I approach two decades on the speaking circuit, I still practice my speeches. First, I spend hours at the computer crafting a speech that fits the occasion and the audience. That's just the start. On the page, my speech is merely a composition of thoughts, ideas, and research. To get the words and phrases to live, I must practice to connect the audience to the content, to transform the message into a clarion call to action. I also have to work on the pacing to keep the interest and entertainment level high and to deliver the desired lagniappe—just a little bit more—that I strive to make my trademark. All that goes on behind the scenes of a performance that's over within thirty minutes to an hour of its start.

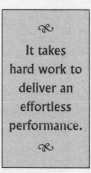

It takes hard work to deliver an effortless performance.

High achievers have a higher mandate for excellence. I now consider myself lucky. I was born to parents who were poor of pocket but rich in spirit. They expected a lot of me and they had faith that I'd always rise to the occasion. As a child, my basic household chores included doing the laundry; folding the clothes and ironing every-thing, including the sheets; washing dishes (no dish-washer); washing clothes and hanging them on the clothesline; dusting and vacuuming; mopping and waxing the floors; and emptying the trash. I had to straighten up the house on a continual basis. Outside I had to pick the pears out of the yard (and we had a huge pear tree!) and sow the seeds for the garden, and then pick the vegeta-bles. There are three girls in my family; I am the youngest. The chores grew as if they were being fertilized, and I didn't get an allowance or special recognition for my work; it was just what I was expected to do to pull my weight.

I also had a newspaper route each morning before going to school. My additional activities were all church-related. In Sunday school class and my youth group, the Buds of Promise, we learned lifelong principles. My organizational involvement actually began in church and my training for speaking was there. All this had to be bal-anced with getting "A's" in school; I was reminded that a "C" would not "see you through." Without ribbons or badges or too many family conferences on the subject, the standard bar was clear. The "A" grade was expected and so it was achieved.

> ❧
> Success in our society is peak performance, not reasons that it did not happen or could not be accomplished.
> ❧

Success in our society is peak perfor-mance, not reasons that it did not happen or could not be accomplished. Consider the bar raised. A young woman engaged in a job search was asked during the first interview

whether she would be willing to work holidays and weekends. She replied that her weekends and holidays were
reserved for personal enjoyment. A second
interview was not requested. Next.

Work ethic is not part-time. It is not
what we do in snippets between computer
solitaire, bathroom gossip, and leisurely
lunch hours. If you have work, work it.
Don't take on-the-job vacations. Otherwise,
somebody or something will replace you.

A work ethic is an asset. Prize it!
Beyond shoring up your job security, there
is a benefit to doing your job thoroughly
each and every day. Opportunity loves a
willing spirit and blesses those who say,
"Consider it done!" more often than those
who say, "It's not my job." While listening to a very high
achiever, I heard some sage counsel. In her career, this
executive had consistently chosen always to do the work
at hand. Notwithstanding the assignment (or assignor)
and her other responsibilities, she decided to treat any
extra task as a learning experience and to let it become a
part of her knowledge base and portfolio. This humility
and hard work boosted her up the ladder in short order.
Her success demonstrates the virtues in just plain hard
work—without shortcuts or complaints.

The last I checked, there weren't any more openings
for job critics. So don't waste your time and talent ana-
lyzing, judging, whining, or sulking. Do become low-
maintenance, strive to become the one everyone knows

> ✃
> Opportunity
> loves a willing
> spirit and
> blesses those
> who say,
> "Consider it
> done!" more
> often than
> those who
> say, "It's not
> my job."
> ✃

he can count on. Perform the tasks of your job with efficiency and expedition, not entitlement. Offer new thoughts and ideas that will benefit your organization. Don't insist. You are an employee, not the employer. There is a difference. When you are self-employed you can set and follow your own rules—to the letter. In the meantime, if you want to feel your soul really sing, carry out your assigned tasks with a generous spirit and a smile. Even if you're not in your dream job, you'll soon realize the truth in the saying that "a smile is a curve that straightens a lot of things out!"

Compare the workplace to a classroom setting. The teacher is in charge—offering information and familiarizing you with the requirements for course completion at the desired grade level. You have the responsibility to learn the culture of the school and classroom. Notwithstanding your brilliance, you gain new insights from your peers as you evaluate theories, formulas, and hypotheses. Even if you have studied hard for a test, count on a connection between what is asked and the actual answers you give in response.

The workplace has a culture that you must learn. All your colleagues can become your teachers and your allies. People respond to people, not directives or mandates. Position yourself inside the loop where valuable information and experience are being shared—whether in the office, in the break area, at the early morning breakfast, on the tennis court, or at the gym. Remember, great teachers, advisers, and mentors appear in many guises. Greet everyone with a welcoming countenance.

Now here's a new job for you: From this moment, you are going to take the starring role in your life. Like all stars, you are going to recognize and cultivate your talents on a daily basis. You will not allow your skills to stagnate. Walk with me now to your talent bank, unlock the door, and throw away the key. The time for hiding your gifts has passed and it will not return. Reflect on how well you speak, sing, sew, perform, clean, write, paint, repair, organize, knit, instruct, cook, create, or lead, and then determine how you're going to take these abilities to the next level. Here are five general guidelines to follow in your personal pursuit of the extraordinary:

Be Bold. Decide to be dogged in following your dream. In the Indianapolis of my youth, not many black students pursued higher education. Most finished high school and found employment. They couldn't afford the time or expense. I was determined to get my college degree, and I was fortunate to have a family that supported my determination. Not having much money, we scraped together what we could, with scholarships including the Elks Oratorical Scholarship, the Midwest Baptist Youth Scholarship, academic and work scholarships from Kentucky State University, a student loan, and my parents working two jobs. The day I left for college, my neighbors and family members, actual and "adopted," were there as the car was being loaded, because a dream was coming true—theirs and mine.

In life, be prepared for those who will question your sanity as you go after a bright idea; just don't start to question it yourself! It's a big beautiful world out there.

See beyond your immediate environs, structure, rules, and regulations that exist. Feel the pulsation of your possibilities. Dare!

Be Courageous. The unveiling of the budding self may be held captive by fear telling you to wait for someone else to see, hear, discover, bankroll your dreams. Couple your daring with common sense. For example, if your dream entails leaving behind a steady paycheck, make sure you embark on your adventure with a balanced checkbook, a clean credit record, and a savings account. Evaluate your cash position, collateral, and ability to make it through the best and worst of times. Either have or plan to have a source of "mailbox money," money that will come to you, literally, in the mail— through rentals or dividends or otherwise—without the need for you to be distracted from the pursuit of your dream. In other words, look before you leap.

Be Decisive. Don't second-guess yourself. You are the general in your army, the captain of your ship, the pilot of your plane, the CEO and president of your life, the master of your fate, notwithstanding who comes along for the ride. You have a choice to keep going forward. Once you have made the decision, use good judgment and keep going forward. The easier path is to deny yourself the opportunities that await. The initial step is the hardest one. Take it.

Be Steadfast. When certain people offer more general advice than hard information, or when they throw cold water on your positive outlook, protect yourself and take their words with a generous grain of salt. If you allow other's opinions and judgments to sway you, you're giving them the steering wheel. Don't allow other people to dominate your desire; they won't have to live your decisions, you will. Be solid in your conviction and in the application of your work.

Be Distinctive. Everyone has a personal signature. The task is to not confuse your style with that of another person, or to allow someone else to dictate yours. Something major is lost in interpretation or imitation. I believe that each one of us has unique God-given gifts to express and nurture. Hold fast to your authenticity.

Start now! There is room at the top, but there is limited space, and a date by which to RSVP. It is your time clock that is ticking. Start putting forth the effort now. Go through the door and up the stairs—to the top! Get up! Get out! Get going!

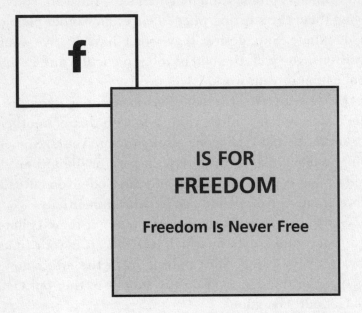

f

IS FOR FREEDOM

Freedom Is Never Free

Freedom is your birthright. It is the birthright of all people the world over, regardless of race, color, creed, politics, economics, or gender. It is a basic human right. Without it, we have nothing, particularly the opportunity to develop our full potential. Freedom is exultation and triumph. It is relief and sanctuary. It means the right to be, to do, whatever one wishes without impeding upon the rights of others. But freedom is not and never has been free.

Call it a salad bowl or a melting pot—regardless of the label, America is a crazy quilt of fiercely independent, self-determined individuals enjoying the invaluable bounty freedom affords. While there are those who take it for granted, for many Americans freedom is not a given: It is precious. Look deeply into the eyes of these Americans and you will see a profound understanding of how much freedom has cost:

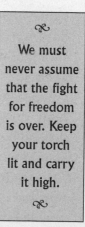

℞
Freedom is exultation and triumph.
℞

- A veteran of World War I.
- A Haitian, Cuban, or Russian recipient of political asylum.
- A professor whose research criticizes the government's policies.
- A survivor of the Holocaust.
- A gay man who is out to his employer.

There are those who would encroach on this invaluable terrain and push back our progress. We must never assume that the fight for freedom is over. Keep your torch lit and carry it high.

In the last few years, international rights organizations have purchased the liberty of thousands of slaves in Sudan at the rate of $55 a head. Astonishing, isn't it? Many people assume that slavery was a thing of the dark, distant past, never to be repeated. Tragically, it remains very much with us. Every day, around the world, tens of thousands are held in bondage, their most basic human right denied, their dignity debased, their humanity despised.

℞
We must never assume that the fight for freedom is over. Keep your torch lit and carry it high.
℞

For generations, America's Statute of Liberty has stood as a cherished beacon of freedom for many oppressed in their own homelands by virtue of their religious or political practice, their gender or ethnic origin. Many were lured to our shores with dreams of streets lined with gold (a legend perpetuated in part by certain U.S. manufacturers seeking to attract cheap foreign labor) but far more simply yearned for a deep, pure breath of freedom. For immigrants, there was a sweet element of "at last-ness" to their search for emancipation. Their existence had been one of daily travel down the road of praying, waiting, hoping, and wishing for sweet release from harsh religious, economic, or social dictates imposed on them by those in power. Their spirits craved freedom.

Freedom should not be a birthright limited to a dominant group or culture. There is not a sprawling front lawn for the powerful and a fenced-in backyard for the rest. America's Founding Fathers instituted a magnificent set of ideals and protections to ensure that our hard-won freedoms would remain codified and preserved through time. As Stephen Carter noted in his book *Integrity*, "Democracy is about making sure that every voice is heard, that no voice is privileged and that everybody plays by the rules." Indeed, the Fourteenth Amendment and its Equal Protection Clause embraces each one "yearning to breathe free." The American Constitution and our rich body of law and jurisprudence put force behind our Founders' best intentions and enabled them to become a practical reality.

For many people, America always has been synonymous with freedom. For others, sometimes tragically, it has not been. For the generations of Africans brought here against their will and forced into slavery, America was not the land of the free and the home of the brave. Nor was it for the generation of Japanese-Americans interned during World War II or for the Americans blacklisted for their beliefs during the McCarthy era, or for generations of blacks relegated to separate and unequal public facilities or for women denied the vote and other basic political liberties, or for early generations of Polish, Irish, Chinese, Hispanic, and German laborers forced to live and work in squalid quarters for starvation wages. For these people, it was a very different land.

It wasn't so long ago that certain freedoms we now take for granted were withheld. Our understanding and our support of the full meaning and possibility of freedom continue to evolve. As our knowledge of this human right continues to become more sophisticated, we must continue to seek out, liberate, and protect those for whom freedom is still just a word. For today, when we consider those falsely accused and imprisoned, or those reduced to living in riot zones where they can't walk the streets past dusk, or those elderly who can't afford proper medical treatment or food, or those young black men who can't walk about freely without arousing fear and recrimination, or those handicapped who can't access a supposedly "accessible" facility, or those denied financing or jobs because of their color, gender, or sexual preference, can we really tell ourselves that their freedom is intact? Can we still truly believe that we are all free?

Freedom does not allow us to distance ourselves from its requirements. We cannot dislodge ourselves and step behind the cover of "someone else" as long as our liberty is not imperiled. As the noble warrior for freedom Dr. Martin Luther King, Jr., said: "As long as one minority is unsafe, every minority is unsafe." Interestingly, we are moving toward a time when our demographic shift toward a Hispanic majority with blacks and whites in second and third order, and thus the image conjured by the word *minority* shall shift and assume a different resonance.

> ❧
> Freedom does not allow us to distance ourselves from its requirements.
> ❧

As the sons and daughters of first-, second-, and third-generation immigrants become more established voices in local, state, and national government, the concept of freedom has changed and will continue to evolve. Perhaps their immigrant forefathers rejoiced over their freedom to hold any political or religious belief and they looked no further. Or maybe the circumstances of the first generation's existence were so demanding, the resources so sparse, that they remained compliant, subservient, and accepting of whatever liberties were extended to them. The second and third generations, however, assume the responsibility for their results, ever building on the earlier struggle and sacrifice and using that momentum to propel them forward toward a more perfect liberty. They find, as Robin Morgan commented, "There is something contagious about demanding freedom."

Experts have discovered that when freedom is denied or deterred, when there are circumstances of oppression, as in the case of Holocaust death camp prisoners or the Vietnam POWs, the survivors relied on a compelling vision of the future to keep them alive. We need an equally powerful vision today to motivate our determination to extend the definition and enjoyment of freedom to all Americans. Here's one possible vision of freedom for all: Everyone is able to find his own niche, have an ease of consciousness, feel productive and valued for his work, freely select friends and associates, speak when he chooses and stay silent at his will, come and go at his pleasure, marry his true love, and have his own way in many situations. Many of us are grateful to live that vision already. Many more Americans can still only dream of it.

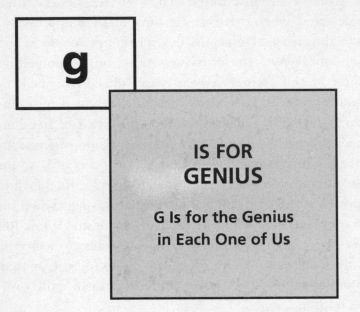

g

IS FOR GENIUS

G Is for the Genius in Each One of Us

Have you ever created something, put it aside, come across it years later, and felt astonished that you were its author? I remember years ago, one spring, when I decided to get down to brass tacks and finally clean out a huge armoire in the guest room. In the bottom drawer, I came across some papers that I'd written in college and law school. (Of course I started reading them; I'd rather do that than clean!) If I'm honest with you, I have to say that I was impressed. I knew more and could articulate it with more authority than I realized. Most of us, most of the time, have richer endowments than we realize or tap.

Moments like these, when you rediscover one of your creations with pleasure, might be God's way of trying to point out our gifts to us.

What are your gifts? What do you offer the world? It's an uncomfortable question, isn't it? Unless you know the answer, though, recognize your gifts, how will you be able to celebrate and share them with everyone else? After all, a gift isn't truly a gift until you give it away.

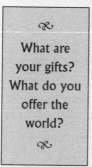

What are your gifts? What do you offer the world?

Recently, someone asked me to pinpoint my genius, and she wouldn't let me get away with just listing my speaking skills. She knew I felt uncomfortable coming up with a list (it felt vain and self-congratulatory), and so she suggested that I ask the people who really know me and whom I trust to describe what they appreciate about me. Let me tell you, it was a surprising exercise! Some ways I thought/hoped I'd impacted them, I hadn't, and other ways I never imagined, I had. It was a fantastic experience. If you're having a hard time identifying your genius, you might want to ask your friends and associates—those whom you trust for their candor and sensitivity, to write down their own thoughts on it and share it with you (you could offer to do the same for them). Do remember, though, that, ultimately, you alone can write and revise your genius statement over time.

Take a moment to get quiet, close your eyes, and put a human face on genius. As you say the word *genius* to yourself, visualize someone or a group of people who embody that word for you. Who are they? What are they doing? How are you responding to this display of genius? Do you feel a deep yearning to emulate their performance? If so, you might now hold a clue to your own hidden talents, a key that will enable you to unlock the chains that have held some of your potential captive and to take steps toward satisfying a deep desire that will make your spirit soar. Your charge now is to travel within, to shake hands with that portion of yourself that awaits your visit and welcomes you home.

> ❧
> To travel within, to shake hands with that portion of yourself that awaits your visit and welcomes you home.
> ❧

Some of you reading this will be quite aware of a great talent that you possess. For you, I have an important message: Don't rest on your laurels, because arrogance and genius don't mix. Remember the story of the tortoise and the hare. The hare, fast and shrewd, was convinced that no one could catch him. He easily won any race. The tortoise, meanwhile, was slow and easily outpaced and thought to be out of his league. When they raced, the hare was inattentive, careless, and complacent. The tortoise kept pace, moved forward slowly but surely, passed the hare and won the race.

I hope it's clear by now that genius is not solely reserved for physicists, chemists, mathematicians, or educators with trained minds that, as I often tell one of my very bright friends, need to be insured. Genius is expressed in countless ways, large and small. It is a type of genius to know what to say and when; it is genius to craft and execute the correct strategy; it is genius to possess deep empathy for another person's plight; it is genius to form and lead a successful team; and it is genius to always remember someone's name. And make no mistake, it is genius to be a role model for children directing them away from the places and people that will impede their progress, and it takes a genius to "know thyself"!

It is genius to recognize that you are not its sole possessor. Think of those who shine brightly without blowing out someone else's candle or who make another person's candle glow brighter. Or those who volunteer their time, touching the lives of others and helping to boost their potential in small and large ways. It is genius to participate in someone else's life.

Florida state legislator Frederica S. Wilson, once an elementary school principal, decided that mentors were the key to helping inner-city boys as they stood at the crossroads between nowhere and opportunity. Ms. Wilson founded the Role Models of Excellence program, in which male mentors whose backgrounds reflect the children's experience—that is, absent fathers or mothers, unemployed parents, substandard housing, chronic hunger, parental illiteracy, societal rejection, and dangerous neighborhoods—but who excelled despite it all because someone cared, lent them a hand, and they grabbed hold. She believed that these mentors, gentlemen who dreamed and overcame, could inspire and instruct these boys. In the program, the mentors are called Peddlers of Hope because Wilson recognized that these children had no hope, did not value their lives or the lives of others, and had no vision of the future. It's worked. Now, when the "Role Models of Excellence" are asked to stand and be acknowledged at a ceremony, the boys jump to their feet alongside their mentors. They have seen the promise and possibility of the future through the experience of these men and now dare to hope the same can come true in their lives. Since its inception, Role Models for Excellence has recruited more than 2,500 men for the program, touched the lives of more than 4,000 boys a year, and won a presidential award and citations. This program was a stroke of genius.

The beauty of this world is that there is room for so many different forms of genius. Frederica Wilson has a gift for matching a societal need with a community resource on a large scale. Others have a variation of this genius on a smaller scale: These folks are the masters at making interpersonal connections, at meeting people from all different circles and walks of life and then seeing ways that these diverse worlds can link together, collectively or one-on-one, to form new, positive links of all sorts—from romantic introductions that lead to marriage, to new patrons who lend needed financial support for a struggling nonprofit, to a new subtenant for a small business owner's idle office space. You might think of them as bees, buzzing from one human flower to the next, cross-pollinating as they go. What a precious gift, especially in an age when we've e-mailed ourselves into isolation.

Yes, we desperately need the genius that inveterate networkers provide. And yet, if people spent all their time buzzing from one person to the next, who would have time to exercise their genius for painting, poetry, needlepoint, woodwork, design, or any other activity that demands some concentrated moments of tranquillity? And if people spent their time creating, who would be left to sort and organize that which was created? God bless Dewey for his decimal system that got our libraries in order.

When I have the opportunity to witness brilliance in an art form, it gives me a real sense of acclamation that makes my spirit scream, "Bravo!" It seemed an eternity that I stood in the New York theater lines to see the much acclaimed *Bring in Da Noise, Bring in Da Funk!* The production was a nonstop tapping explosion on hardwood. It was a magical experience whose genius inspired me.

> ❦
> The beauty of this world is that there is room for so many different forms of genius.
> ❦

Genius comes in many shapes and sizes, and there is no true hierarchy. Yes, someone who can shoot a three-pointer from half-court can probably command more money than someone who can come up with a mean rhyming couplet; however, money is not the true measure of worth.

Think of a need that was prevalent in your community until an entrepreneur did the homework and filled the void with a convenience store, upscale restaurant, dry cleaner, or shoe repair. It required his willingness to stop, think, and apply his mind to the situation while taking a risk to accomplish the goal. Think about where any community would be without the basic services that visionary entrepreneurs establish.

> ✃
> Genius comes
> in many
> shapes and
> sizes, and
> there is no
> true hierarchy.
> ✃

Your genius is as unique as your signature; it is that personal trait which causes others to announce your accomplishments with an exclamation point. Your wisdom, knowledge, experience, exposure, perception, retention, charisma, and rough edges too; your long strides and small steps; your responses to fears and apprehensions, joys and sorrows, gains and losses, strengths and weaknesses equate to your stroke of genius. One person shows genius by keeping in personal contact, her business thrives; one person consciously seeks to remain creative while being highly productive, he is successful; and a hospital receptionist operates a hands-free telephone operation, dealing with a new caller about every thirty seconds, responding to each one's needs while staying calm and being courteous. What is your special signature? Make sure to add your genius to the world today: It will make everyone richer.

Expressing your genius can take courage; sometimes you'll have to carve a path when there seems to be none. Have faith. Believe that you can apply your mind to the matter and reach your level of genius. Your genius is flawless. Use it.

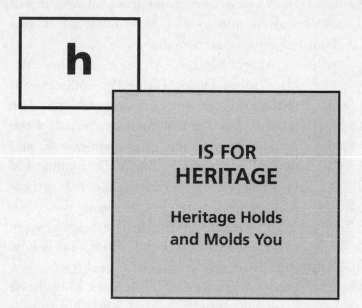

h

IS FOR
HERITAGE

Heritage Holds
and Molds You

Wherever you go in life, you are not walking alone; your family is with you. Whenever you walk into a room, you can throw your shoulders back and hold your head high, for you represent the proud experience and expression of generations of people. Consciously or not, they helped to mold and shape your appearance, personality, and intellect.

Whatever your station in life, be mindful that where you came from is not necessarily where you are going. But where you end up is tied to the honesty you give to your beginning. Sooner or later, living in a world of make-believe will catch you. Avoid the past and it will find you. You cannot outrun a lie. Find the good in your life. Acknowledge your past and grow.

> ∽
>
> Where you come from is not where you are necessarily going.
>
> ∽

Mom, Mother, Momma, Mutha, Ma, Dad, Father, Daddy, Da, or Pop connects you to the ancestral line of your family tree. The multiple branches of the tree consist of the grands, great-grands, great-great-grands, and beyond. A long, strong line of those connected by a beloved, blood relationship. A heartbeat that sounds through each generation.

The extensions from the branches are twigs, the siblings. The brother that is now irreplaceable, the sister that is now your best friend. Yes, maybe when you were growing up in the same household, you swore to yourself sometimes that you would never speak to them again because they just didn't get it! Today, you can't imagine what prompted that passionate pledge. With the passage of time, they seem sane, and you are satisfied with their improvement.

Think of the times you have heard it repeated that some particular conduct is expected, even accepted, because someone in your family did the exact same thing. Maybe you laugh until you cry over the same jokes that would tickle your mother, or you cock your head when you listen intently just like your grandpa did, or you hum to yourself as you walk down the street like your dad. Each and every one of us possesses in our own ways this rich evidence of our heritage; it's our family's fingerprint on our lives.

Of course, there are also those less subtle genetic manifestations that make a complete stranger conclude, even without DNA testing, that someone's physical characteristics make him or her undoubtedly part of a particular family. It could be in the spectacular height they all share or their "big bones" or small frame or high cheekbones or violet eyes or stick-straight hair or curly hair or, my favorite, that deep irresistible dimple on the left side of their face. It's as though each family member is a small part of one gorgeous tapestry that was designed to be together.

I invite you to wrap yourself in all of your heritage. Think of it as a warm, enveloping quilt that gives you strength and comfort to make it through even the most trying times. Think of it as a brightly colored flag that announces your history and roots to all who approach you. Know that it is a great and honorable legacy that you'll leave behind for your children and grandchildren.

> Wrap yourself in all of your heritage. Think of it as a warm, enveloping quilt that gives you strength and comfort to make it through even the most trying times.

Did you grow up hearing stories about where your family came from and how they strove to survive or thrive and what they have achieved? One friend of mine had heard some snatches of family history and lore. From her grandmother, she understood that she might have been the descendant of a renowned writer, and she heard that another ancestor was the first missionary to go outside Europe. Her parents, though, always played down their heritage; they felt it was vain and superfluous to dwell on the family history. So my friend grew up without a firm sense of her roots and often lacked a sense of belonging, of her place in the world. As she grew older, she was determined to get a sounder footing. She decided to take a genealogy course so she could fill out her family tree and understand her origins and spiritual inheritance. As she embarked on this adventure, a wise friend warned, "Be prepared. You'll find horse thieves and horse owners, Presidents and paupers." She persevered, knowing that, for better and for worse, her heritage is the one and only sure thing she will ever possess.

What can you do short of starting a preservation society? A good place to begin is to cultivate the childlike sense of wonder that asks, "Why?" about all aspects of your family history. In your next phone conversations with close or distant relatives, old or young, strive to learn more about them and their knowledge of your shared origins. Ask them about their favorite holiday tradition, swap family legends, discuss shared values, make plans for a family gathering. Begin the journey together through past lives, through the hopes, dreams, fame, infamy, struggles, and sacrifices of your ancestors—through all that forms the pure groundwater of your present.

Be sensitive to even the smallest traditions that distinguish your family from another. Perhaps the man of the house always prepares pancakes on Saturday morning. Or maybe you always took one camping trip each summer to a national park. Or it could be the Sunday suppers you shared at the "big house" after church. At each life transition—the departures, arrivals, births, mar-

riages, divorces, and deaths, take care to bring these ritu-
als along with you. Don't abdicate all of them to those of
your in-laws or new companions: Preserve some, blend
others, and form new traditions to leave behind. Fads
vanish. Traditions remain constant.

Start collecting: pictures, quilts, souvenirs, recipes,
books, china, letters, and all the things available from
family members who will share. Capture your oral tradition for prosperity. Create video and audio recordings of
the reminiscences of young and old, separately and together. I've seen some of the
most beautiful exchanges unfold between
the most senior family member and the
baby. The quizzical child clearly enamored
with the wisdom embodied in those who
have lived more than a moment, coaxing
the elder's long-dormant memories into the
light; the youth's faithful retelling of his
day-to-day adventures—the capture of his
first firefly, the first ride without training wheels, the first
visit to the petting zoo—sparks the elder's fresh recollec-
tion of his own pleasures of youth.

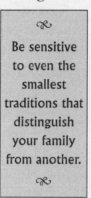

Be sensitive
to even the
smallest
traditions that
distinguish
your family
from another.

Is there a family member who excels at interviewing
others—perhaps a lawyer or a journalist by training?
Enlist that person's help in drawing out each family
member and encouraging each one to recall all the dear-
est individual and shared family memories. Many people
feel uncomfortable talking about themselves but will
warm to the task if they see that others really care
enough to ask and to listen.

Think about making your next family gathering a special potluck supper. Ask each relative to bring a covered dish made from a "secret" family recipe. Offer a door prize to the family member who uncovers and creates the oldest family recipe. Offer another award for the person who has the best story to tell about the dish. The special garlic spread, fried-corn spoon bread, three-alarm red bean chili with buffalo wings, smothered greens or old Indian pudding literally will refresh your family's memories. What better way to start the conversation, get the recollections and fun flowing, and celebrate your family's unique heritage! Make sure to bring your camera.

In retrieving the memories of yesterday, you can find the best-kept secrets of your ancestors. While standing in the concrete of the past, you hold an admission ticket to all the subtle mysterious notes that serve as guideposts for the future. Today, it may not seem like a major accomplishment, but in the 1950s, it was. My aunt and uncle operated a premier sit-down restaurant that was the Sunday choice for after-church dinner, with white linen tablecloths and waitresses in white uniforms. You could not get a seat easily. This was a no-nonsense business operation that was kept immaculate and had great food and a jukebox, as well as a myriad of variety items that attracted young people. Additionally, businesses ordered takeout lunches throughout the week, the baked goods were award-winning, and the ambiance was perfect for meeting and greeting. My aunt and uncle were early entrepreneurs; from their example I learned the value of hard work. I also learned that when you are self-employed you are simultaneously in administration, sales, repair, and, as the saying goes, "chief cook and bottle washer"!

Touchstones to your family heritage probably fill your home. Think about all the irreplaceable things—the old photographs, your great-grandfather's ship clock, your grandma's cameo pin, your aunt's favorite yellow felt fedora hat with the genuine ostrich feathers, your brother's soapbox derby trophy, your mother's lace handkerchief, the pressed flower petals in the old book, your uncle's old fishing rod and creel. These are the things we treasure most, which have value beyond measure. They connect each of us to precious memories (the fishing trip that the men of the family took together one summer), culture (the faded samplers and quilts that our women stitched in sewing circles), pride (the good set of china dishes and the white linen tablecloths), homesteads (the pewter candlesticks that lit our ancestors' dining tables), faith (the religious books with each new marriage and birth faithfully recorded in ink) and legends of our family through its many generations. The intrinsic value of these items cannot be weighed on a scale, counted in dollars and cents, or even kept securely in a safety deposit box. They grow richer with time.

> ✂
> In retrieving the memories of yesterday, you can find the best-kept secrets of your ancestors.
> ✂

In these transitory times, our jobs, retirement, and dreams move us from place to place. With each move, there is a temptation to pare down and simplify and leave things behind with the old house. As you do this, take care to judge the full worth of each item. Make certain that the old book or locket or school desk that you are thinking about quickly discarding as sentimental or mere excess is not actually a keepsake that will help your progeny recall an important family milestone. Even the smallest item that appears to be valueless can, on closer inspection, prove to be priceless, because of when and why it was made or purchased or a sacrifice that it represents.

> ❧
>
> Even the smallest item that appears to be valueless can, on closer inspection, prove to be priceless.
>
> ❧

Whenever she's facing a tough day at work, one woman I know puts on two touchstones that remind her of the tenacity and courage that are part of her birthright: an antique coral cameo and Chanel No. 5. Both were passed on to her by her grandmother, who was a very strong-willed, never-say-die lady long before it was popular and who prided herself on being a "Birthright Free and Fighting Quaker" (those Quakers who split off from their pacifist brethren and fought in the Revolutionary War). As she dons the perfume and the heirloom jewelry, she feels as though she is carrying the inner strength and conviction of her ancestors onto the corporate battlefield.

So far, we've been perched on the family tree. Even so, there are those who've figured large in all of your lives, who form part of your heritage, who don't appear on the tree. Think of your extended family with its godmothers and godfathers, honorary aunts and uncles, and your own close-knit community of dear friends, teachers, mentors, counselors, consolers, neighbors, supporters. In short, think of all those who took the time to give instruction, to notice when you were being extraordinary or foolhardy. They paid attention and helped you to decide when you were unsure. They have always been there for you, concerned and paving the way for your smooth access to higher ground.

Once we moved across town, Reverend and Mrs. James L. Cummings were our neighbors. He became a Christian Methodist Episcopal bishop. I was asked to baby-sit for their daughter, Denise. This family nurtured my thirst to read and shared their wealth of books. I was given a full and much-sought-after opportunity to read from their library and explore the ideology, works, and writings of numerous writers. Reading took me places, expanded my mind and thinking, and gave me vocabulary and conversation beyond my years.

Life has its twists and turns. A noted theologian was giving his sermon and said that he was told, "Well things could be worse!" He cheered up, and "things got worse!" For those rough places, I've been especially grateful for those members of my community who've helped me to find the good in the bad. Like my extended family members, Reverend G. A. Brooks, pastor, Caldwell AME Zion Church, who would let my sisters and me go into his office and read his books and periodicals and tell us Bible stories; Mrs. Lucille Dobbins, who directed my path toward higher education; Mrs. Virtea Downey, whose home was used by me and other children after school to do our homework and prepare for youth meetings at the church; Mrs. Veanie Dawson, who helped to place me on the national scene in the community of faith as she was a staunch educational leader at the national level; and Mrs. Lula Mae McCampbell, who guided me in the direction of college to her alma mater, Kentucky State University, and who helped to ensure that as a first-generation college student I would obtain necessary scholarship awards. My extended family would not be complete without Jarnell Burks-Craig, who has been a helping hand, willing arm, and always-there-for-me shoulder at every stage of my life. They attested to my ability to accomplish what seemed impossible, because they had consciously made the decision to believe in me. They loved me unconditionally, even when liking myself was a challenge. They and others like them also form the bright lights of my legacy.

They loved me unconditionally, even when liking myself was a challenge.

Take time to protect and nurture this part of your heritage too. Think about the concept of investment and return. School administrators and teachers did not believe that the now acclaimed educator Jaime Escalante could prepare poor Latino students to pass the test for advanced calculus. They thought that if the students could master fractions they would be doing well.

But he appealed to the students' sense of heritage, reminding them that the Mayans discovered zero. This success story resulted in the film *Stand and Deliver*.

You can't expect to constantly make withdrawals and

no deposits. Stop now and write a letter to a loving supporter (not an e-mail, make a nod to the past) and let
this person know of your appreciation. Pause to say
thank you for the loan made to you when your financial
ends did not meet and your cash balance hit rock bottom; or when he responded to your early morning or late
night collect call with good advice; or traveled to some
nearby or distant place in acknowledgment of your success or failure. Your handwritten letter will strengthen
the connection and will project the depth of your gratitude and respect. "Thank you" is simple; say it and mean
it, then show it. Make time each week to
pick up the telephone, give greetings, and
check in on their well-being. You can do it
at any time—don't wait until you need
something or to share once-a-year holiday
tidings. Answer the call to connection now!

> Take time
> to rediscover
> your birth-
> place and to
> explore the
> birthplaces
> of your
> forebears.

In addition to family and community,
setting also determines an element of your
heritage. Take time to rediscover your birth-
place and to explore the birthplaces of your
forebears. Visualize your life as a puzzle
with many pieces. Find the old family home and yard,
seek out the country meeting house with its old wooden
pews, go to the local cemetery and read the stone mark-
ers, spend time in the town plaza, talk to the town's residents. Embrace this environment that helped to form
you and your ancestors.

A big part of my summers in childhood were spent in
Kentucky and took place in a small, white wood-frame

church that perches off the side of the main road. The parking lot was anywhere on the grass where you chose to park your car—which always produced some confusion on a regular Sunday morning and even more when the church swelled past capacity for a revival, wedding, or baptism. There couldn't have been more than twenty pews in the whole church. The piano wasn't grand, and it could have undergone a thorough tuning. The choir tried. When the temperatures soared as they often did in the hot days of summer, our air conditioning was the reliable hand fans from the local mortuary, and when they did not do the job, the double doors of the church were opened to get a fresh breeze and to welcome the flies.

Whenever I return to Kentucky, for a regular visit or for a special occasion, I usually spend some time at this church. As I listen to the same gorgeous hymns that touched my young spirit, memories—happy and sad—flood back. I remember all the people who touched my life and passed through those same doors. Most of all, as I rest my back against the hard wood pew, I know that I am truly home. I feel at one with the most noble parts of my heritage.

When you go home or gather at a reunion, look for clues to the mystery of your life. That person standing across the room may have influenced your commitment to stand tall, look your listener in the eye, and remain focused on the agenda. Someone else may know a cousin who shares your same smile. Take time to collect the revelations from your past. Don't run. Crawl. Make it a point to discover in minute detail everything that there is to learn. Build on your findings.

Be sensitive to the essays of those ancestors who took little and did much. Whenever you start thinking that you don't have the resolve or the perseverance that others have demonstrated, your heritage says, "Yes, you do." Just pause and reflect on the experience of generations past, and you will discover that you are equal to the test. It's inescapable. It's inside.

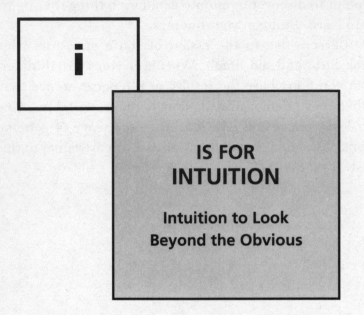

i

IS FOR INTUITION

Intuition to Look Beyond the Obvious

Your intuition is your all-natural, built-in thermostat signaling change. It senses opportunity and danger, truth and falsehood, right and wrong. Nudging you with a sudden, sharp feeling of "heads up," it helps you to apprehend and respond to shifts in your life. It's your job to check it regularly and to heed the message on your private radar screen.

Think of the times, more than a few I'm sure, when you have answered the telephone and the person already in your thoughts is there on the other end of the line. Or think of the occasions when you instinctively got in your car and drove to a friend or relative's home in the belief that person needed or wanted to see you. Upon arrival, you discover that this friend just had to undergo a battery of medical tests and is nervously awaiting word on the results. These coincidences always amaze us at first. When you think about it, though, your instincts probably were designed to help you stay "tuned in" to your extended family, even when you are miles apart. Perhaps intuition is intended as a natural call and response system that keeps you "on line" with your loved ones. (Word to the wise: Intuitive impromptu visits are not popular with kids in college, if you know what I mean.)

Our five senses of hearing, sight, touch, taste, and smell are vital to our receipt, processing, and transmittal of information about our environment. Our sixth sense, intuition, is a precious, life-enhancing feature that works with the other senses to keep us from being harmed. This attribute acts as a check on the data perceived through the other senses. For instance, if the words you hear don't correspond with the speaker's body language, then your intuition will send you a warning signal. As your gut senses a false positive, you'll choose or refuse to act, approach or move away cautiously, ask questions or withdraw in silence. You may then turn to a network of trusted friends to sound out

> ⸙
>
> Intuition is a precious, life-enhancing feature that works with the other senses to keep us from being harmed.
>
> ⸙

your choice and get a reality check on your hunch, feeling, or foreboding that another time might be more fortuitous. Your friends may even suggest that you need to just pass altogether.

If you ignore your intuitive sphere of attention, awareness, and astute observation, you can miss the opportunity to maximize that which is innately yours. There are times, for example, when silence is golden. Your sixth sense wisely sends you a message to listen and learn. Other times it might urge you to take immediate action. Your intuition tells you to make the investment, you wait, and the price soars. Boat missed.

Be of good cheer, guys, intuition is not for women only. A male colleague told me that, in the midst of his two-week vacation, he traded in T-shirts and jeans, sand and beach, and the quiet of being away for the maddening demands of telephones and faxes, suit and tie and office chaos, because intuitively he knew that some things needed to get done. His intuitive force pulled him back to the office to find a pipe that had broken, his executive assistant on emergency leave, and three stacks of "Urgent" materials on his desk, one of which was from a grantor advising him that a major grant had been funded. He was right to return to the office, this time, but not every time.

Learn to feel the pulse of your perception. If your heart seems to skip a beat, it could be a sign that you're being falsely led by another. If your mind seems to be running on overdrive and you can't articulate your thoughts, your intuition will kick in and urge you to slow down and think, because you're moving too fast to operate in your own best interest. If your feet start voluntarily plodding along, instead of briskly walking at your regular clip or your usually legible penmanship is scrawled over the page, take notice, the writing is on your Intuitive Bulletin Board. Slow down.

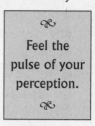

ભ
Feel the
pulse of your
perception.
ભ

Dr. Eugene Genlin, author of *Focusing*, states, "You can train people so they have the capacity to get a hunch anytime they want one." He offers two steps:

- Heed certain body sensations to feel how an idea sits physically.
- Even if the idea produces an uneasy feeling, focusing on it further for a minute or two will help you discover what is causing the agitation.

Remember traffic lights have three signals: red, green, and yellow. The yellow light indicates a need for caution, and that's one that your intuition often flashes. Early in your relationships, in particular, you're wise to heed the yellow signal, trusting your head to discern slowly the other's purpose first, and then listening to what your heart tells you about this new acquaintance's true intent.

Actually, even as you progress in your relationships, it's wise to bring your intuition along. One man increasingly felt pangs of fear each time the phone rang, he answered, and the caller hung up without a word. He also noticed, but downplayed, his spouse's disinterest in his activities and her monosyllabic utterances. She did seem to have a renewed zest for her job and she started to work longer hours. But each time he felt an inkling, a wait-a-minute, he chastised himself for being paranoid and distrustful. Of course, when he returned home one day and found the closets empty and half the furniture gone, he felt blindsided when really he'd been blind.

Intuitive moments also provide vital information about a pending situation. How many times has a quick vision of a future event flashed through your mind, alerted you to take a certain action, and you dismissed it instead? How many times have you found yourself later regretting that disregard? Interestingly, meteorologists give thorough weather predications grounded in science, yet they are periodically confounded by the totally unexpected driving rainstorm, tremendous wind shift, or hurricane. Before leaving for work one day, an aging uncle reported, "It feels like there's going to be a major storm." Rather than double-checking the weather report, I ignored his intuitive observation altogether, left without a raincoat, and suffered the flu for the next two weeks.

Many times, we ignore our intuition or that of another because we wish to deny its flashing lights of danger. We don't want to hear the message. A friend of mine was in a job that was not a good fit with her skills or personality. With each passing day, she became more and more miserable. Finally, another employer came along and offered her a job that sounded too good to be true. It was. Even during the negotiation for the position, her friends saw warning signs and pointed them out to her. For instance, the would-be "white knight" offered one salary and bonus, then backed out of that offer and extended a less generous compensation. He agreed to her benefit package request but refused to put it in writing (saying that it would be an informal understanding)—of course, he reneged once she was on board. Ultimately, she found herself working for a man who played fast and loose with federal trade, accounting, employment, and immigration laws. She'd leaped from the frying pan to the fire because she'd refused to heed her intuition or that of her closest friends. (P.S. That company was taken over and dismantled—the boss fired, her job lost.)

In the workplace, where most of the important rules are unwritten, your intuition is an invaluable navigational device. Use it to read the climate—tropical or arctic— and then steer your passage. In a crowded room, intuition can pull you like a magnet to the powerbrokers, where the conversation can impact the bottom line and your future. It can guide you to contributing in team meetings, nudging you to speak up or to keep your own counsel. It can suggest whether a phone call, e-mail, fax, or face-to-face meeting will get the desired result. And it can help you to anticipate which trends are worthy of action to help you jump the curve ahead of your competitors.

You can mistakenly confuse intuition with mind reading. It is not the same, and it's important to keep the two distinguished. Let's say you conclude that your spouse is angry because you ran up the credit card. Or maybe you think your colleagues don't like you because they didn't ask you out for happy hour after work. That's not intuition; at most, those may be false assumptions. In both instances, your intuition may have been on alert, trying to indicate to you that something was amiss. To reach a more specific understanding of the situation, though, you needed to do more spade work to collect more concrete information. Be careful not to confuse intuition with fatalistic thinking: The first will boost your potential, the second will sabotage it. Assume the worst will happen and it often will.

The more in tune you become with your intuition, the more you use this additional information to guide and protect you, the more serene you will feel. To exercise your additional sense or range, it is not necessary to develop a special dragnet for trouble, disruption, confrontation, or mistrust. You do need, however, the security of knowing that you will not choose to refuse or ignore your first thought out of hand. If your sixth sense keeps telling you to take a real vacation instead of a few days off, carefully evaluate this suggestion. Think through what it would mean to go out of town and stay there instead of remaining "hooked" to all of the needs, real and imagined, imposed by the office. Or if your intuition tells you that your child is distancing himself from you, collect more information. Gently ask him how he's feeling and test the possibility that you've become estranged. Your intuition combined with his will help you to name the problem so that you can tame it.

Did you set the alarm? Is the garage door down? Are your keys in your pocket? Did you turn off the iron? Did you forward your telephones to your answering service? My intuition says that you did! Don't think that your intuition is there to nag you, bore you, bother you, upset you, or confuse you. Instead, your intuition will place you at the fifty-yard line with the play book for the plays before and during the game. Intuition is being surrounded with that which makes just what you were thinking real, not imagined. Use your intuitive sense. Pay attention; your voice is speaking. There is a narrow space between your voice and your inner voice. Listen.

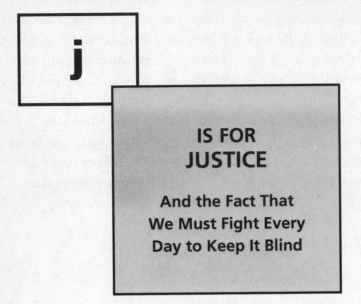

j

IS FOR JUSTICE

And the Fact That We Must Fight Every Day to Keep It Blind

Justice is a woman, blindfolded and balancing scales. She doesn't evaluate skin color, gender, sexual preference, religion, or creed before meting out her decision. Unfortunately, she is a statue, and few humans can emulate her stolid impartiality.

We do not wear blindfolds but we are all blind to the true worth of another. One friend told me that each of us is like a beach ball with all different stripes of color. Yet when one person approaches another, she can see only the red and yellow stripes, and that's all she perceives of her acquaintance. Only God can see the whole picture and is aware of the full range of potential that each and every one of us offers the world. Assume there is always much more to someone than meets your eye and act accordingly.

Fear is one way that our relationships are limited. We allow fear to construct vicious, pat stereotypes in our heads. We attach a certain meaning to a person's skin color, accent, gender, religious observance, mode of dress, height, and so on. Then we grant or withhold, listen to or ignore, trust or distrust based on that unjust filter of that person's merit. As a black woman, I am very sensitive to prejudice based on skin color. It's destroyed the lives of too many people that I know, respect, and love. At the same time, I myself am not innocent of discrimination. For example, when I hear a British accent, I assume that the speaker possesses above-average intelligence and sophistication. This has led me, in group settings, to listen more attentively to the contributions of the English participants—irrespective of the actual value of the insights offered by them or my American peers. Granted, this particular prejudice might be considered relatively innocuous; even so, it leads me to live a lie and it gets in the way of a just world. Regardless of its guise, prejudice is wrong and poisons our society.

> ❧
> We do not wear blindfolds but we are all blind to the true worth of another.
> ❧

In conversations on the issue of justice, race, equality, and fair play, favorite and repeated phrases are "I'm color blind" or "I don't see color!" or "I don't care whether you are white, black, brown, yellow, green, or purple. Color does not matter to me!" I would argue that it matters to us all. I would also argue that black people don't want to be purple, green, or white. We do not strive for erasure. Like others who suffer discrimination, we hope our children will arrive at a place where people can regard one another as they are—color, gender, culture, creed, and all—without ambivalence or reticence. Then there are no barriers, only bridges. Justice advances in the public or private sector when people are celebrated and when we treat them the way we want to be treated. A Native American proverb states, "Don't judge any man until you have walked two moons in his moccasins."

> ❧
>
> People can regard one another as they are—color, gender, culture, creed, and all—without ambivalence or reticence.
>
> ❧

We all have to strive to overcome fear. Fear keeps you on the narrow path of sameness and refusal to accept difference. Fear will not let you appreciate the culture, creed, and customs of people unlike yourself. Fear builds cages and keeps you housed in a tight cubicle, missing out on true friendships, acceptance, and sharing that could have been. Fear stagnates. Get past fear and watch your horizons expand and your spirit rejuvenate.

Think about the business term *value-added*. It is a plus, meritorious and worthwhile. The opportunity to get to know, appreciate, and spend time with people of different countries and cultures, in my opinion, is a "value-added" process. Diversity adds a rich cultural mixture to our lives; we all gain insight into the struggles, sacrifices, and perspectives of different people. When I was a student at Howard University School of Law, Washington, D.C., Andrew Young—who headed the U.S. Mission to the United Nations—came to our campus and reminded us that we should get to know our classmates. He cautioned us to treat them well and wisely, for one day they would occupy leadership positions in this country or others around the globe. He was right.

Imagine being at a reception where all the guests are having a very good time. They are comfortable with people just like themselves—either by race, gender, socioeconomic class, rank, or department. People do not tend to walk across the room and introduce themselves to someone outside their own group, because they fear rejection, being viewed as an alien. They don't want to be identified as a perpetrator or an intruder on closed turf or, perhaps worst of all, to be judged a "brown-nose."

A new employee at a company's annual holiday party was eager to meet and greet everyone there. In a short while she was deeply engaged in conversation with a gray-haired gentleman to whom she was expressing her views about the company, her supervisor, her team, and work flow. It turned out, of course, that he was the chairman and CEO. Had she known, she wouldn't have ventured to his side, much less engaged him in candid conversation! On a positive note, he has never forgotten her name.

Recently, I was at a crowded reception, and only one person was racially different. Until I approached him and talked with him, he sat alone. No one was willing, it seemed, to bridge the gap, even under the guise of social graces or hospitality. He was, in fact, a great conversationalist, informed about and interested in many contemporary issues. I was truly pleased to have the opportunity to sit beside him for the rest of the evening. Nothing ventured, nothing gained.

A white person asked me how she could overcome her fear of minorities. She told me that she wanted to know "them," notwithstanding her fears. (She was honest, most of us are not.) My answer to that question is to open our eyes and observe "them," whoever they may be. Pretty soon, we'll see that people are people. They celebrate and they hurt. They love and they hate. They're bold and they're afraid. In the main, they have or enjoy few entitlements or endowments. They put their shoulders to the wheel and work to achieve, or they idle. Similarities in hopes, dreams, and initiative are far more prevalent than not.

Yet, with more than a slight consistency, I have been denied, twofold. The reasons relate to race and gender; in common parlance, I am known as a twofer. There's a perception that my career has benefited from this dual "minority" status. For people with that perception, I understand: It is much easier to think that I was handed my opportunities than to acknowledge that I was the best qualified. It's easier, but wrong, to doubt just what can be accomplished by a woman—black or otherwise. The day I was promoted to the chief of my branch at a federal regulatory agency (back in the days of my legal career), one of my senior staff attorneys told me that he would rather work for a black than a female. Realizing his dilemma, I asked him, "Which one do you think is going to change?"

Fear and prejudice are not the only factors that pervert justice: privilege, selfish greed, political corruption, and jealousy also play havoc. Someone once said that privilege extends to a small number of people a rich cache of unearned assets, a weightless knapsack of special provisions, tools, maps, code books, emergency gear, and blank checks, while others, even with a lot to offer, are denied access to mainstream participation. This uneven playing field discourages the young, who may assume the dice are loaded against them, and breeds dangerous anger, distrust, and resentment among people of all ages. We all must strive to deal fairly with others in all aspects of our lives, to lead with our hearts and heads.

> ❧
> The problem with society is never over there. It's always right where each one of us stands.
> ❧

The problem with society is never over there. It's always right where each one of us stands. So look at where you are today and ask yourself, "Am I just?" "Am I thinking of doing what's right, or am I only trying to get my way?" "Will my next words promote harmony and balance in this situation, or breed jealousy and acrimony?" "Do I cede the conversation to the views of others, or do I stand up for what I believe?" "Am I putting any action behind my vision of social justice?" Be reminded, silence is not golden; it is destructive. Speak up! Speak out!

Ready or not, things will shift as we approach the twenty-first century: The minority will become the majority. Let's take steps now to make sure this change is one that's for the better of all mankind. Early lessons about people from all walks of life are critical for our children. Let's teach them, now. If children becomes adults without a sense of unity and justice, without an innate rejection of hate crimes, without intolerance for repression, they'll lead lopsided lives. They're destined to lives of strife, not harmony.

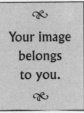

You can promote blind justice by looking at the very thorny issues of our society and becoming a part of a diverse community focus group. Share your opinions with the other group members honestly, temper the discussions by having a facilitator; otherwise, you will waste valuable time. Pay attention to the attitude you bring to this conversation and others. Do you have a scowling face, a cocked head, a hand on your hip when you are taking a position, a caustic voice when you are arguing for or against a sociosystemic issue? Your image belongs to you. Does it please you? Is it open and inviting, does it express the willingness to give another a fair hearing?

In life, I take comfort in my faith that the scales of justice will bring balance to all circumstances and personalities. I truly believe that "the wheels of justice grind slowly, but they grind exceedingly well." At times, you may feel as if you have a disproportionate portion of hardships, have suffered more than your share of negative aberrant behavior, and have gotten too much of that which is bitter, not sweet. As you measure the intensity of your difficulty, take care not to wallow therein; rather, turn the power of your mind and purpose to ways that you can contribute to the solution rather than the problem. Be encouraged; justice is not forever lopsided or imbalanced. Justice will not be denied.

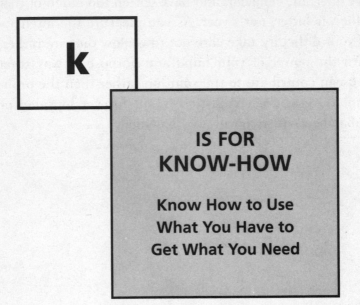

k

IS FOR
KNOW-HOW

**Know How to Use
What You Have to
Get What You Need**

The French have an expression for it: savoir faire. The literal translation: *savior* means to know and *faire* means to do. It suggests more than sheer intelligence; it connotes finesse; it says that its possessor can wield her wisdom to great effect; it purrs action.

Have you ever heard the expression *book smart*? When I hear that, I figure it means that someone has a head chock full of facts and figures but hasn't the slightest idea how to use it. Knowledge without know-how remains stuck on the shelf; it doesn't get past go.

Know-how is a combination of knowledge, experience, observation, flexibility, and initiative. Watch a high achiever and you'll see someone who doesn't give up easily, who learns from her own mistakes and who tries a new approach. She knows that you always have to consider all strategies to capitalize on what life offers. She is most likely to say, "If the door is closed, I'll go through the window." And she is most likely to get where she is going.

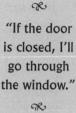

&

"If the door is closed, I'll go through the window."

&

While know-how is critical in all aspects of one's life, it is particularly vital in the world of work. In the workplace, those who lack the savvy to know that these days everyone's job extends well beyond the description handed to him at his initial interview, will find themselves quickly left behind those who are cognizant of all the requirements of modern, fast-moving companies. At one Fortune 100 company, for example, it's understood that the systems engineers will "just fix it." Regardless of the problem or the instigator or even their prior experience with the situation at hand, they are charged with having the know-how to get the information, expertise, and/or parts needed to take care of the problem. Engineers without the initiative, flexibility, and maturity to take charge of whatever the day dishes out need not apply to this company. In varying degrees, the same expectation is held for all of us in most workplaces.

Experience shows us that know-how always resides on a firm foundation of education. Education introduces you to a common body of knowledge that others will assume you share with them as the jumping-off place for your conversation. In the absence of studying subjects of universal reference for those who've attended high school and college, one would feel confused and left out of the flow of the discussion. Then too, of course, in certain trades and professions—such as architecture, medicine, law, and mechanical trades—you are powerless to carry out fundamental aspects of the work without first receiving specialized educational training. Think about it, would you be comfortable if a gourmet chef had the assignment of leading a tactical maneuver for the armed forces without any training?

Many young people, as they're curled over their math books studying cosines, fail to see how education as they know it could have any practical application in life. The seeming lack of relevancy can lead them to talk themselves out of applying themselves to their studies or, worse yet, can lead them to thinking that dropping out won't make a big difference in their lives. I always encourage the students that I mentor to stay in school without interruption. I sympathize with them that the tedium of a particular semester can make a temporary break from school—perhaps using it to travel to world, take a full-time job, get married, or engage in myriad other activities—can seem more enticing and worthwhile. Invariably, though, I point out that these detours generally stretch long past their welcome, derailing further studies. The students then find themselves with a shaky database in a world that demands smooth and speedy handling of all information. They might even find themselves stranded on the sidelines. I try to help my protégés realize that there's time enough to experience the world; first gain the education the world expects, then make the grand entrance.

Once upon a time, most people got their college degree and went to work and they didn't have to worry about adding to their educational base. Now all of us are engaged in continuous improvement of ourselves. Among other things, we all need to constantly train ourselves to use new software applications. Others must take continuing education courses to retain their industry credentials that indicate they are competent to provide services in their respective fields. Another part of the drive to stay ahead of the curve comes from the more stringent requirements of our heavier workloads (in the wake of reengineering). And with the restructuring of much of corporate America in recent years, we've all come to realize that we have to keep ourselves attractive to potential new employers since job shifting is the rule rather than the exception. We must have the know-how to flow from one opportunity to a new one.

An important question to ask yourself and to answer honestly: Do you define yourself by your job title? Do you think of yourself as a labor lawyer or a print journalist or a textile purchasing manager? Or do you think of yourself as a problem solver, a wordsmith, a deal maker? Beginning to define yourself along the lines of your skill sets or the specific aspects of your know-how will help to open your eyes and your attitude to the diverse number of attractive career opportunities that could present themselves to you. It could put you on a much faster track to accomplishing all your life goals. Remember: The road to the top is not always straight up from where you are standing right now.

If the past is an indicator, the future will be unpredictable. Therefore, having the opportunity to develop and exercise skills that will prepare you for any sudden shifts in "the way things have always been" is to your advantage. In the decade of the nineties, one of the most repeated words was the Big "E"—*Empowerment*. The word has been prevalent, powerful, and thought-provoking. Empowerment means to act from your own vantage point, to have firsthand information and know-how, and to be in a ready-set-go posture.

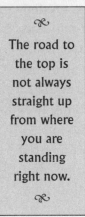

The road to the top is not always straight up from where you are standing right now.

Start now to develop the know-how that will take you to the next level. Take time to study the doers and to learn from their example. Figure out why they seem to be able to run circles around everyone else. What do they tackle first? Are they detail-oriented? Do they delegate? Do they spend much time explaining their actions? What makes them tick? To whom do they turn for help? Don't be in such a hurry to arrive at your next destination that you fail to observe and soak up all that your current stop has to offer you. Good things do come to those who wait and watch!

Ask for help. Sometimes I have reverted to my bad old habit of trying to do it all by myself, thank you very much. I usually am not even conscious that I'm doing it, it's such an automatic, fallback position for me.

Sometimes I have to try repeatedly to do something, fail at it a few times, and tire of banging my head against the wall before I remember to use that simple four-letter word: HELP! Next time you find yourself thinking in frustration that there must be an easier way, look around you for a helping hand. Undoubtedly there is someone who knows how to do the task faster, more easily, or with less hassle. Know-how also means knowing when to leverage off someone else's know-how!

Consider these guidelines that have worked for me when trying to decide whether I should persevere or ask for help:

- If you don't have the answer immediately, ask yourself, "Should I be able to answer this question or handle this situation on my own?"

- "Have I done everything possible and used all the resources available to me to resolve the situation?"

- "Do I have time to try again, and is my customer/boss/peer willing to wait for it?"

- "Is this situation over my head? Does it require more authority?"

These questions can also reveal those times when, in a moment of weakness, I was about to give up out of frustration. They force me to get back on the horse and make another attempt.

Assuming that you're got all your immediate job responsibilities under control, volunteer to take on an extra project. Jump at the opportunity to do something beyond your expertise (unless it would harm you or others). Always strive for continuous improvement in your prescribed tasks. Know-how comes from stretching yourself, from trial and error, from exiting your comfort zone and moving forward. As a wise man once said, "Bad judgment leads to bad experience. Bad experience leads to good judgment."

Every time your life is not running according to plan, think of it as an opportunity to try something different, to amass some more know-how, to flex your brain. Imagine finding the office elevator hung with a sign that reads, much to your dismay, "Out of Order" or "Closed for Repairs." What to do? Take the stairs and enjoy all the benefits and realities therein—such as climbing at your own pace, exercising your legs and lungs, depending only on yourself. In the beginning you may not be able to see the top of the stairs or you may think that you will never reach your desired floor. As you proceed, your physical stamina may surprise or dismay you. You may have to hold on to the rail, take modest steps, and even ask for divine intervention. Remember, there is probably a reason that you've been given an opportunity to try a different way, and it's probably not because you need to practice your whining technique! Accept your circumstance, take the action before you, and ask others to lend you a hand. You'll be astonished to see how much farther you'll go.

Your challenge in the twentieth century, as I see it, is to remain active, engaged, and instrumental in every area of your life. If you don't "use it," you are sure to "lose it" in a time when the premiums go to those with enough savvy to go with the flow. Stand ready to engage either the analytical left side of your brain or the creative right side. Strive to work in an industry and environment where you face fresh challenges and have room to grow. Do what it takes and take what you can from each new opportunity. Be the one in the know.

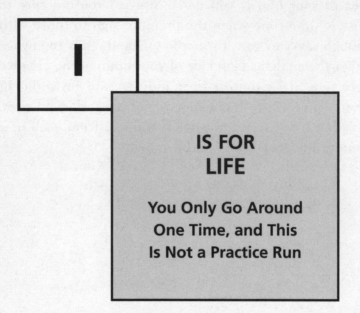

I

IS FOR
LIFE

You Only Go Around
One Time, and This
Is Not a Practice Run

Wouldn't it be incredible if you could freeze-frame all your most enjoyable moments in life? I would freeze-frame learning how to hopscotch and how to beat my friends at yo-yo. I would freeze-frame learning how to ride a bike without training wheels. I would freeze-frame the excitement of my annual visits to the state fair and the circus where I rode the Ferris wheel and the merry-go-round and stood in never-ending lines for my favorite food on the planet, popcorn. I would freeze-frame the relief I felt when my swimming teacher reassured me that I could not drown because my own buoyancy would keep me afloat. I would freeze-frame the day I finally purchased my first car and moved from driven to driver. Which moments would you freeze-frame?

Cherish your sweet memories. Look back, but don't stare. Don't freeze and stay rooted in past pleasures. Instead, move ahead to the next adventure. Don't wait.

Have you heard that "Life is what happens while you're making other plans"? (Or its variation, "If you want to make God laugh, show him your plans.") In relative terms, we are only on this planet long enough for a cup of coffee. If we wait around for all circumstances to be exactly to our specifications before we decide to make our next move, the moment is lost forever. The path to frustration is paved with lots of elaborate plans and little execution; it keeps us paralyzed, between where we are and where we want to be. Take a step now, in any direction. Don't wait.

> ❧
> Cherish your sweet memories. Look back, but don't stare.
> ❧

I would rather be ashes than dust! I would rather that my spark should burn out in a brilliant blaze than it should be stifled by dry rot. I would rather be a superb meteor, every atom of me in magnificent glow, than a sleepy and permanent planet. The proper function of man is to live, not to exist.
I shall not waste my days in trying to prolong them. I shall use my time.

Jack London

Do you have your life on hold? Are you waiting for one of the "if onlys"—if only I could lose twenty pounds, or get a new job, or find my Prince Charming, or have more time, or move to the perfect neighborhood, or buy the right car, or get more work done—to come true? The longer you wait, the longer you'll wait. Seek correction not complaint. If you need more time, learn time management and get organized. Meet every challenge with action. Don't postpone joy. Get out and start enjoying life now!

For those of us who are dedicated to our careers, we must remind ourselves on a regular basis that LIFE is more than work. Life is more than besting the competition, getting over and through, clearing the way to the top, climbing over and on someone else. Life is more than crafting the next strategy to generate a guaranteed revenue stream or to reduce overhead costs.

Life is having a true friend and being one. Life is a walk in the park on a brisk winter day. Life is walking in the rain. Life is seeing the sun rise and set. Life is opening a letter from your favorite aunt. Life is getting a physical examination and learning that all is well. Life is being in the stands for your grandchildren, children, nephews, or nieces and watching their code sign just for you acknowledging your presence. Life is taking water aerobics and feeling your heart beat and your muscles tire. Life is riding in the car with your nephew after he's passed his driver's test.

In short, living life to its fullest means being prepared to capture the opportunity of each moment, to recognize all the possibilities given us to join with our community and grow, and to venture beyond our own mental backyard. As many have testified, no epitaphs have ever read: "Didn't spend enough time at the office." Will yours read: "Didn't spend enough time having fun?"

> *The man who views the world at fifty*
> *the same as he did at twenty has*
> *wasted thirty years of his life.*
>
> Muhammad Ali

In one period of my life, without being aware of it, I went three years straight without taking a vacation. I was so focused on career and community and giving both my all that I didn't take time to refresh and recharge my batteries. I couldn't relax and take time off just to be: Each and every trip was a working trip. I only snapped out of it when I noticed that I felt less joy, my life felt colorless, I had the chronic blahs. Luckily, I recognized the signs, knew that I needed a true respite, and forced myself to take a complete vacation from all distractions. Only when I reached the vacation resort was I finally able to put the fast-forward, machinelike schedule of my life on pause. I was so exhausted I literally didn't leave my hotel room for three days. All the resort's accouterments of comfort and entertainment were put on hold; I had done too much for too long.

Open your eyes to a new reality with time to go in slow motion. If a time clock were placed on your life for 365 days and no more, how would you live your life?

Would you make any changes? Would you recall things forgotten, brushed aside, or hidden, and assess them as being—more valuable.

I learned my lesson. Now I take my pleasure wherever and whenever I can. As a professional speaker, I travel around the country nonstop. Rather than just focusing on the speaking engagement, I try to take a little time each day (if only a half-hour or so) to take in the local sights. It's been marvelous to walk down Chicago's Magnificent Mile; experience the incredibly fast pace of New York City; partake of the sheer beauty of the changing fall season in Connecticut; take a ferry ride from Vermont to Potsdam; soak in the moss-draped charm of Savannah; gaze at beautiful, snow-capped mountains in Denver; savor conch fritters in Nassau;, shop in Hong Kong; or stand in Cape Town and have a sense of déjà vu.

Don't wait. Don't wait. Don't wait.

When I visited my father's nursing home for the first time, I wondered why many of the residents did not acknowledge my greeting with a smile or a simple hello. In the cafeteria, I was surprised to see an attractive woman who seemed much too young to be a resident. Most residents were at least seventy years old; she didn't appear to be more than fifty. As I studied her face, I kept wondering why was she there. Then I looked beyond her face. She had no lower extremities; she was a double amputee. Gradually, as reality set in, I recognized why the other residents hadn't spoken to me or anyone else. Many suffered paralysis from a stroke, others had lost their hearing or sight, still others had lost both, and others were lost to senility. Most were living in days bygone. Don't wait.

It may come as a great surprise, but we all have our share of ups and downs. You do not have a monopoly on either the good or bad things that can and will happen in your life. Therefore, don't whimper or get bogged down with complaints. Life is not for handholding; it is for living.

Start living your full purpose today. If you continue to remain tuned to the outside world, responding to each new crisis and urgency with no thought of tomorrow, if you make no time to look within and acknowledge your inner desires, your goals will remain fragmented and your dreams dashed. You will have a feeling and, ultimately, a resentment for arriving at your final days lacking a sense of completeness and satisfaction. You'll have only yourself to blame.

Start a journal to capture your deepest desires and dreams and to begin planning their realization. Record your feelings and the most important passages. The blank pages are waiting to be filled with your innermost thoughts and episodes. When you put your experiences in writing, you breathe oxygen into your every day. You disallow all of life's occurrences to evaporate into thin air. Instead they are written, defined, and have structure. They become your treasure. Journal entries can paint a picture for you. Imagine a canvas and that you have a brush; with its stroke you can create the content and design and you can provide the interpretation. This is your private, personal submission of your thoughts, ideas, hopes, dreams, aspiration, ups and downs. This is your record of being uptight and having days when you "hung loose." Your journal is much more than a script in a play. It is quiet whisperings to yourself, and you are gatekeeper of all that is within. By writing, you engage the convergence of fact and fiction and see your progress in its unfolding. This, your journal, is your catharsis.

> ❧
> Life is propped up with bookends: grace and mercy.
> ❧

Your existence is rooted in that which is spiritual and longs for cleansing of the soul. Some experiences will make you look back and question your stamina and arrival on the other side of a problem or a situation. But somehow, you made it. Others will confirm your suspicion that life is propped up with bookends: grace and mercy. Standing on either side of our human experience, grace and mercy surround and protect us, guide and guard us irrespective of our actions. When you chronicle the events of your life and you do not feel proud of all that has transpired, you are still forgiven. These bookends help you through life's tough and difficult places.

Seizing life is as important in the small moments as it is in the large ones. Once, I was in San Francisco on Nob Hill waiting for a much delayed cable car, and I decided to walk down to Union Square. It was more like skating than walking, given the steep incline of the hill. Being adventuresome, after my shopping tour, I decided to walk back up the hill to my hotel. The effect was analogous to Chinese hot mustard sauce to my sinuses and lungs as my allergies and short wind made each breath a labor. But I

walked, block by block. That's what life is, skating, climbing, working, striving, trying hard to make it, and feeling
a sense of affirmation in saying over and over again, "Yes,
I can do this!" One word says it all: "Yes."

As a credo for your tomorrows, know that the points
in the game of life are not the reason you play it. Step up
to life's realities, win, lose, or draw. You learn from every
encounter. Life is not about a roll call of whom you
dated or married or whether you were ever married or
raised children. Life is not about whether you were
manor-born or poverty-stricken or somewhere in between.
Life is not about the color of your skin, hair, or eyes. Life
is not about the fraternity or sorority to which you
belong or whether you chose to pledge. Life is not about
status and things.

Life is about you and your evaluation of yourself. Life
is about building bridges of friendship rather than burning them. There are too many bridges to cross. Life is
about showing concern and compassion while you bathe
in happiness and satisfaction. Life is about replacing
anger with calm and hate with love. Life is about avoiding
jealousy, overcoming ignorance, setting aside stubborn-
ness, and building confidence. Life is having a sincere
purpose. Life is about seeing people for who they are and
not what they have. Most of all, *most of all*, life is about
choosing to use your life to touch someone else's life in a
way that could have never been achieved otherwise.

Choices are what life is all about. On your mark. Get
set. Ready. Go. The first duty of life is to live.

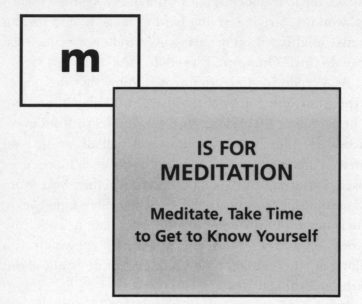

m

**IS FOR
MEDITATION**

**Meditate, Take Time
to Get to Know Yourself**

In any major mall in America, you will find a directory
indicating, among other things, the location of department stores, specialty stores, beauty services, and food
courts. The chart also always has a bright circle or
square that says, "You are here."

No matter where you're headed, your journey begins
right where you are standing. And the first step is to take a
look at where you are today. Look at your attitudes and
your behaviors. Consider carefully the risks you're taking
and the resolutions you're making. Think about the condi-

tion of your relationships with others and the community. Then ask yourself, "Are my thoughts and actions a reflection of my truest self?" Such daily self-assessment is what you can and must do; otherwise, you are always operating within the boundaries drawn by another craftsperson.

In meditation, you are given the opportunity to stand still, collect yourself, listen to the silence from within and know that you are here. Right now. And in this moment, you have absolutely everything you need.

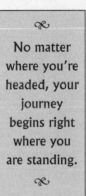

No matter where you're headed, your journey begins right where you are standing.

Slowing down and spending time in quiet reflection each morning can lead you to a life filled with clarity, direction, serenity, and the most profound joy imaginable. And yet, we live in a society that values speed and constant activity above all else. So we've placed our lives on fast-forward. The clock radio blasts us out of bed and into the shower. We grab a cup of high-test coffee and wolf down a muffin and then race out to face another jam-packed day. After doing, doing, doing until we can do no more, we race home to beat rush hour (as if only one hour a day qualifies for that name) and then drift to sleep with the radio or television playing in the background. This we believe is a full life, the good life. Yet true goodness, a truly rich life, is the mirror reflection of all that.

The key to the real good life can be yours for free. Just listen. Turn off the TV, the radio, the coffee grinder, the washing machine, the telephone, the fax, the can opener, the computer, and sit in complete silence. Slowly but surely, your soul's deepest yearnings will step forward and show themselves. They will point the way to a life more fully lived. All you have to do is listen, trust, and direct your feet on the sunny side of the street.

I know how scary it is to sit quietly with absolutely nothing on the agenda if you've never done it before. Before I began a regular practice of meditation, I felt that any minute not filled with some activity was a minute wasted. Many years of packing as much as possible into each and every minute eventually took its toll. After rehearsing points I wanted to make in a business discussion, my mind would go blank shortly after the discussion began. There would be mornings where I couldn't remember whether I had grits or cereal, or even bothered to eat breakfast at all. I would go into a room to get something and then forget why I had gone there in the first place. I had a hard time staying focused on a lecture or a sermon in church. I even forgot to make time to phone my birthday greetings to loved ones. I felt burned out and out of control.

I'd read and heard a lot about the healing benefits of meditation and I knew that I had to try something different. My candle was close to being extinguished. So I set aside half an hour one morning to sit quietly and reflect. I only made it for five minutes. As soon as I closed my eyes, all these voices in my mind piped up. "You should be doing this." "Why haven't you taken care of that?" "When are you going to get around to . . ." Well, you know the drill. It wasn't a pleasant experience, and I thought maybe I wasn't cut out for meditation. Maybe it only worked for other people.

Friends encouraged me to keep trying, though, assuring me that they'd had the same experience when they first started their meditation practice. After several more attempts, I found that there were different ways that I could reach the peaceful meditative state. Sometimes, if I just ignored all those voices, they eventually went on their way and I was able to get in touch with a more profound being. Other times, I would acknowledge any feelings of pain or joy and calm my spirit by expressing empathy for my humanity. Still other times, I would put on some relaxing music and let it carry me toward a serene state. And then I've found that allowing my fingers to gently caress a stone can help to ground me in the here and now. All it takes is willingness, commitment, and a decision to make a little time for myself each day.

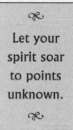

Let your spirit soar to points unknown.

If you feel as if you've been burning the candle at both ends, juggling family, work, community, and church, and not feeling particularly satisfied with what you have accomplished, take time to renew your spirit. Turn off the electricity, light some candles, and watch the glow. Let your spirit soar to points unknown. Relax your mind and body by letting all the "urgent" items on the itinerary vanish. In meditation, there is no hurry to get finished. There is no clock ticking. No alarm will go off signaling that now you must return to business as usual. You deserve a break. Take it.

When you hear the word *meditation*, do you think of sitting cross-legged in an incense-filled room while chanting "om"? In reality, there are as many different ways to add the meditative practice to your life, to pull your spirit upward and outward, as there are people. A university president friend of mine took me to his place of thinking and mediation. As we climbed a winding stairwell to the roof of the campus administration building, he cautioned me that security had warned him to stop going up on the roof, because they were not convinced of the safety of doing so. He was, however, convinced of how renewed he felt after each visit. For it was there that he could see for miles, without obstruction, the university's place within the community and could envision his dreams for the school and his life. There too he found he was able to lay his burdens down and feel real peace.

Other friends have found that nature calls them. They find peace in the mountaintops or gazing contemplatively toward the heavens. I have one friend who loves snow. She'll watch through the windows as it slowly blankets the land with magnificent and pure beauty. And sometimes she bundles up and takes a meditative stroll through the snowfall. In these moments, she feels closest to her divine purpose.

Here's a meditative practice you can try the next time it rains. Focus your attention and take note of the rain as it falls. The pitter-patter has its own rhythm and comfort. Take advantage of this chance to release your thoughts, clear your mind, and enjoy deep cleansing breaths in time with the rainfall. For an even deeper slice of peace and harmony, close your eyes and listen to the rain so that you can receive your spiritual gifts.

You can extend the benefits of your morning or evening meditation practice with a few other conscious changes in your daily routine. In the morning, for instance, you might chose to jump-start your day with a long walk or run rather than coffee. Some people have found that this routine boosts their energy level, gives them the chance to think through challenges and opportunities, allows them a chance to have a conversation with their god, and helps them let go of any pent-up stress. Then, during the day for the next thirty days or so, you might decide to refuse the invitation to associate with people or things that turn up your stress level. Measure the level of added peace you feel in the before and after and judge whether you want to institute this practice on a continuing basis. At night, you might take time to curl up with a good book that does not require you to be an ambassador, advocate, or analyst. Rather, select from the multiple choices of those inspirational authors who give encouragement, ways in which you can find deeper self-assurance and affirmation.

Here's one last meditation exercise for you: Imagine that you are the executive producer of the movie of your own life. You are in charge of being in charge. You can cast yourself in every role of the production, from director to editor to scriptwriter to casting director to choreographer and even wardrobe manager. Now, with you in charge, what would that movie look like? Whom would you include in the film? What would you edit out? See what clues this production can give you about the gifts you can celebrate in your life, as well as the places where you might make room for new prosperity.

Meditate. Make time to take time to get to know who you really are. Put aside the telephone lines—one, two, and three—and the faxes, computers, e-mail, beeper, cellular phones, and pagers. Then, shhh! Be still.

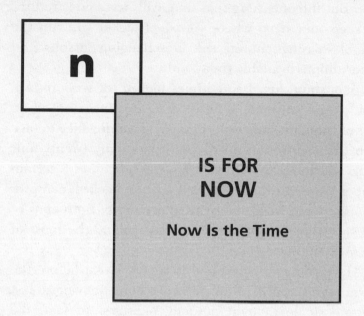

n

IS FOR
NOW

Now Is the Time

In Chapter L, we looked at the importance of opening our hearts to living life passionately, and in Chapter M, we appreciated the value of taking time to nurture our souls. This brings us to N, now. Now we are refreshed, centered, and ready to make each minute count. And now is the time to fasten our seat belts as we get ready to learn how to make the most out of each and every day.

Take a crash course in right now. There is magic and mystery in this very moment. In our VCR world, it's very easy to slip into the notion of pause and replay or do over. But the one thing that time will never do is return. So keep your head where your feet are or you run the risk of missing out on the life-changing lessons and opportunities available today, only.

As a youngster, I sometimes looked for ways to "kill time"; now I'm most interested in stealing more of it. Part of becoming an adult, I guess, is coming face to face with the reality that all of us receive only twenty-four hours in each day. With that realization comes a certain time-is-wasting urgency that, if left unchecked, can propel us straight from inactivity to overdrive. Both ends of the spectrum can prevent us from making the most of the moment before us.

Have you ever awakened in a cold sweat before the alarm even sounded? Your mind is reeling, moving so fast that no single thought actually registers. In fact, the sheer velocity of your thoughts only serves to fan your panic more, and you feel like a top that's about to spin out of control. In your fear-stricken state, you can't see the first frost of winter, you can't ask your loved one what the day holds for him, you can't offer your children encouragement before they catch the bus, you can't stop to greet your colleagues at work, you don't notice the sales opportunity that comes your way. You are not present because fear has pushed you into the passenger seat and pulled down the visor.

Once I worked with a very high-energy woman. To all appearances, she looked like a high producer: always on the go at top speed. She believed that she worked harder than the rest of the department combined. The reality was much different. She was like a dragonfly nervously flitting across the surface of life. Her fear of the future and inability to tune in to the moment, kept her running in circles, unable to move forward in any meaningful way. Her colleagues gradually discovered that projects took twice as long when she was involved because she couldn't settle down and see her share through to the end. She would alight, get a small portion done, and then feel compelled to rush off to another perceived urgency. Ultimately, she rushed off to another job at a new company, leaving only chaos behind as a souvenir of her tenure.

The next time you feel your mental wheels start to spin, push the pause button. Take a deep breath, close your eyes, and place your hands on the edge of the table in front of you. Keeping your eyes closed, describe to yourself what the edge of the table feels like. Is it cold or warm, smooth or sharp, slick or coarse? Next, open your eyes and describe to yourself exactly what you see in front of you. What is the color, the shape, the size? Does it remind you of anything else? Likewise, move on to employ your sense of hearing and then smell. Once all your senses are engaged in sensing the here and now, your heart rate will slow down, you'll feel a sense of ease, and you'll reenter the present. It's the only meaningful place to be. It's the only real place to be.

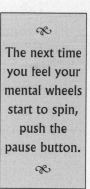

The next time you feel your mental wheels start to spin, push the pause button.

Now that you're here, make every minute count. To that end, let me urge you to get into the habit of sticking with the winners, not the losers. Whether in friendships, professional relationships, or romantic liaisons, you need to align your flight pattern to the right flock. When you're in the right present company, you know it because you find yourself soaring with little effort. If, on the other hand, you feel stuck, frustrated, and negative about future prospects, look at whom you're associating with and ask yourself why you've chosen these running partners (and why they've chosen you!). Remember, when you are working toward a positive end, you need to be with people who are on the same page, with the same mindset, focused on the same goal, not on conflicting minutiae. Stagnant waters stagnate.

Do you love your life today? Or do you find yourself daydreaming about the past or wistfully looking ahead to the future? If you notice that your head is anywhere but in the same room with the rest of your body, maybe it's time that you took an inventory of your life, the way it is, right now. Only by facing your life exactly the way it is right now can you take the steps to lead yourself to an even brighter tomorrow. As they say, "If you can't name it, you can't tame it." Here's a personal inventory that I encourage you to take right now:

Reality Checkup

Name: _____ Date: _____

Directions: Read the "hint" listed below each question and then circle the word to the right of each quality that comes closest to describing how you exemplify it in your life today. If you feel there's room for improvement in this area of your life, read the "suggestions for improvement," commit to those changes that feel right for you, and draw up your own ideas for change under "my next step."

For example, under "are you authentic," if you answered "never," think about the fears that are keeping you from speaking and living your truth. As a next step, you might make a commitment to tell someone honestly what you want to do when asked rather than answering that question with "I don't care, what do you want to do?"

As you complete this survey, remember to be both honest and gentle with yourself.

1. Are you authentic?

Always   Often   Sometimes   Never

Hint: Evaluate whether you tend to be true to yourself in thought, action and deed. Do you say what you mean and mean what you say? Do your actions reflect your deepest beliefs?
   Suggestions for improvement: Use "worst-case" scenarios to help overcome the fear that stands in the way of being truthful to yourself. Get positive support.

My next step: _____

2. Are you a change agent?

Always   Often   Sometimes   Never

Hint: Evaluate whether you take initiative to make a positive difference in your environment.
Suggestions for improvement: Get involved with a
group whose vision touches a deep nerve. Look for
ways that you can contribute to the welfare of others
on a daily basis.

My next step: _____

3. Are you an effective communicator?

Always   Often   Sometimes   Never

Hint: Evaluate whether your technological, verbal, and
written skills will equip you to communicate on a
global level in 2000.
Suggestions for improvement: Prioritize the skills
needed (whether it's word processing or speaking
Spanish), enroll in a course, and practice, practice,
practice. Consider joining a local Toastmasters or
writing group.

My next step: _____

4. Are you community-minded?

Always   Often   Sometimes   Never

Hint: Evaluate the strength of your support network.
When facing a problem, do you think "we" or
"me" as you look for a solution?
Suggestions for improvement: Look for new
opportunities to connect with like-minded people.
Get active and make friends with those who share

your interests. Take a moment each day to call someone else just to see how that person is doing.

My next step: _____

5. Do you have faith?

Always   Often   Sometimes   Never

Hint: Evaluate your level of faith in a Divine Being. Do you most often feel a serene acceptance in your daily life, or are you more likely to feel fearful, angry, and restless?
Suggestions for improvement: If you haven't found a faith that fits, don't give up. Keep exploring, and you'll find your spiritual home. Seek out spiritually fit people and find out how they came to believe.

My next step: _____

6. Are you committed to your family?

Always   Often   Sometimes   Never

Hint: Evaluate your knowledge of your cultural and historical identity and origins. Also judge whether you commit the right level of time to your family.
Suggestions for improvement: Plan family gatherings and seek out the experience of the youngest and oldest members of your clan. If your biological family is not a healthy one, think about creating a new, healthy, surrogate family for yourself.

My next step: _____

7. Do you give back to society?

Always   Often   Sometimes   Never

Hint: Evaluate the amount of time you devote to service.
   Suggestions for improvement: Shift one hour a
   week from TV to charity. Talk to your family members
   and find out if there's a charity you'd like to "adopt"
   and for which you'd do group service work a few
   times a year.

My next step: _____

8. Do you hold grudges?

Always   Often   Sometimes   Never

Hint: Evaluate whether you're able to forgive and forget.
   Suggestions for improvement: Pray for your
   enemies and wish them Godspeed. Remember that
   your resentments harm your spirit and leave the
   target of the grudge unscathed. Don't allow others
   to live in your head rent-free.

My next step: _____

9. Does fear get in your way?

Always   Often   Sometimes   Never

Hint: Evaluate all areas of your life wherein you harbor fear.
   Think about the situations and personality types and
   institutions to which you respond in a fearful way.
   Consider where you'd be today if those fears had not
   directed your actions.
   Suggestions for improvement: Try out worst-
   case scenarios on each fear. Push outside your
   comfort zone and face each fear little by little.

Visualize the positive outcome that will result from facing your fear and taking the necessary action despite it.

My next step: _____

10. Do you challenge your mind?

Always   Often   Sometimes   Never

Hint: Evaluate whether you engage your brain on a regular basis. Think about how often you actively try to learn new things.
Suggestions for improvement: Each week, set aside at least a couple of hours in an activity that gives your mind a workout (e.g., read intellectually stimulating material, attend a lecture on a subject of interest, match wits with another person, or even fill out a crossword puzzle).

My next step: _____

11. Do you feel motivated?

Always   Often   Sometimes   Never

Hint: Evaluate the degree to which you are a self-starter.
Suggestions for improvement: Remind yourself that action motivates, analysis can paralyze. Make a commitment to take one step in a forward direction on a project that's important to you. Check your attitude and, if it's negative, focus on all the reasons you have to be grateful today.

My next step: _____

12. Are you financially secure?

Always   Often   Sometimes   Never

Hint: Evaluate your earning and savings position. Do you
      keep a prudent reserve that will cover your basic living
      expenses six months forward? Are you happy with your
      standard of living? Will it take you where you want to
      go? Is it enough?
      Suggestions for improvement: Look at where you
      spend money and how it benefits you and others. Ask
      where you can save, how you can make more money,
      and who will appreciate this change. Figure out how
      much money you need for your prudent reserve. Pay
      down your debt and resist the temptation to
      accumulate more. Decide what level of wealth is
      enough for you.

My next step: _____

13. Do you deny yourself anything?

Always   Often   Sometimes   Never

Hint: Evaluate whether you indulge each desire or whether
      you withhold satisfying them.
      Suggestions for improvement: Before acquiring
      something new, ask yourself if it's a true need or a
      want. Buy needs and resist many or all of the wants.
      Here, spiritual growth rather than self-deprivation is
      the idea. Often, our desires for material things mask
      our spiritual hunger.

My next step: _____

14. Do you have a good self-image?

Always   Often   Sometimes   Never

Hint: Evaluate how much you like yourself. Pay attention to how you talk to yourself, the stories you tell about yourself to others.
Suggestions for improvement: Create a list of assets and liabilities, with at least one asset listed for each liability. Cultivate a balanced view of yourself. Seek opportunities to do things that will build your self-esteem (such as charity work) and to surround yourself with positive, supportive people.

My next step: _____

15. Are you sensitive to others?

Always   Often   Sometimes   Never

Hint: Evaluate how mindful you are of the needs and concerns of others.
Suggestions for improvement: Call friends and contacts just to see how they're doing. Ask about their well-being first in conversation. Listen to what they are saying when they are talking rather than mentally composing your witty repartee.

My next step: _____

16. Are you serene?

Always   Often   Sometimes   Never

Hint: Evaluate your fundamental sense of acceptance that everything is exactly the way it is supposed to be.
Suggestions for improvement: Keep a firm perspective on your place in the world in relation to others and the Divine. Take time to meditate. Refuse

invitations from drama queens who want spectators for their theaters of chaos.

My next step: _____

17. Are you spontaneous?

Always   Often   Sometimes   Never

Hint: Evaluate whether you leave enough open spaces to capture the spur-of-the-moment entertainment and opportunity. Are you open to exploring new places and things?
Suggestions for improvement: Stop scheduling your life as though you were a locomotive. Leave openings for the unexpected to enter. Pay attention to your heart and say yes to a spur-of-the-moment plan that makes it leap with joy. Ask if fear is standing in the way of more adventure in your life.

My next step: _____

18. Are you task-oriented?

Always   Often   Sometimes   Never

Hint: Evaluate your success at starting new projects and bringing them to completion.
Suggestions for improvement: Keep one project open on your desk at a time. Put it away before commencing the next one. Do first those things you'd least like to do.

My next step: _____

How did you do? Where you surprised in some areas, reassured in others?

Are you inspired to take your life in a new direction now? The steps you wrote down give you the road map to make the piecemeal changes that will take you where you want to go. Just remember that you don't have to take every single step today: You do have to do something now!

My friend Sue found that she had become very serious and fearful. She had started her own business and she was determined to succeed quickly and to not let anyone down. As her mind filled each day and night with bills to pay, customers to call, projects to start, and employees to manage, she found it hard to have her old sense of humor and playful spirit. She was rarely "in the moment." Her friends commented that she needed to leave more room in her life for fun and adventure, that she needed to lighten up, but Sue felt so worried and burdened with all her responsibilities that she didn't know how to begin. Finally, our friend Nan suggested that she place a happy childhood picture of herself on her nightstand, remember how much fun she had in that moment as a child, and make a commitment each morning to do something for herself to recapture that spirit each day. She did, although at first she felt it was a bit silly and self-indulgent. Eventually, though, looking at herself as a happy child each morning filled her with joy, lightened her heart, and encouraged her to believe that everything would work out. Best of all, this shift in attitude prompted her to draw up a modified business plan that would allow her to succeed, lead a balanced life, and be present to what each new day offered.

You determine the quality of this moment. Make it the best one possible. Keep ever mindful of these words from Dr. Benjamin E. Mays:

> *You only have a minute*
> *Only 60 seconds in it*
> *Forced upon you, can't refuse it,*
> *   didn't seek it, didn't choose it.*
> *But, it is up to you to use it.*
> *You must suffer if you lose it.*
> *Give account if you abuse it.*
> *It is just a tiny little minute*
> *But your whole future is in it.*

Catch this moment. It won't be back again. Permission granted. Now, right now, is your time.

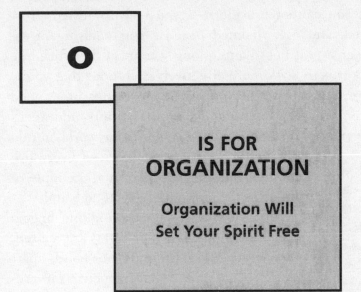

O

IS FOR ORGANIZATION

**Organization Will
Set Your Spirit Free**

Step outside yourself for a day and evaluate how you handle your time. It did not fly away, but where did it actually go? You may conclude that you need better planning and organization, which will enable you to take better care of yourself. If too much time, or any time, is spent frantically looking for your eyeglasses, car keys, that special piece of jewelry that you feel naked without, your planner, or even your briefcase, you have wasted time, and you need to make a change in the way you do things. Money can buy a timepiece but not one moment of time. Get organized; you won't regret it.

Every day, your same level of excellence is expected, and you cannot provide it if you feel exhausted, frustrated, and overwhelmed because you're disorganized. The answer is not to put in longer hours at the office; the answer is to work more effectively each hour that you're there, and that's where organization comes in. A good system will save you seconds, minutes, hours, and weeks of time in all aspects of your work. You do the math. Thirty seconds saved every five minutes adds up to more than a couple of hours at the end of the day. It adds up!

> ❧
>
> The answer is not to put in longer hours at the office; the answer is to work more effectively each hour that you're there.
>
> ❧

Place a rubber band around four fingers on both hands. Now your hands are relaxed, there is no stress. But pull your hands apart as far as possible. What happens? You create space and resistance. Regrettably, time does not expand and you may feel stressed because it does not. You must use it or lose it. It does not stand still or allow itself to be repeated or retrieved. Time insists that you do it now.

There is not one magical, cure-all system for organization. The secret is to have a system that you stick to consistently, day in, day out. One of my friends, an advertising director, swears by her steno pad and pencil. Every time she comes up with a new project or task, it goes on the steno pad. When a project is completed, it's crossed off. It's that simple and it works for her. Another friend of mine, a road manager for bands, takes out a legal pad and each morning writes down the ten things he wants to accomplish that day. He tackles the most important one first and works on it until it's done, crosses it off the list, and moves on down the list. Still another friend, a sales representative, totes her agenda around with her everywhere she goes. She makes it her central database capturing all her appointments, notes, contact numbers, favorite restaurants, and shopping lists in one place. And then there's a lawyer friend who went from paper system to a hand-held computer that he claims has changed his life. The point is that there are different organizational systems at different price points for different personalities. Any one of these can work for you, but none of them will if you don't work it.

The first thing you must do is select a system that you know you can stick with for a long period of time. Take care not to develop one that is so elaborate and complex that you get overwhelmed and give up. Observe the systems that your most organized friends use and then do a trial run with a version of one of those systems. For instance, some of the planner companies have a thirty-one day leaflet that allows you to try out their system of organizing for one month for a modest cost. Or you can mock it up. The idea here is not to go out and sink a lot of money into a system that might not fit with your style. Try it on for size first—for a week to a month—and then make an investment in the one that best suits you.

Now that you have a planner, make a promise to yourself and keep it that you will no longer write on scratch paper. It is very easy to write a note on the back of a pad or on a piece of paper that you have convinced yourself you will retrieve in just a few moments, but there is an interruption, then you mislay the piece of paper, and you spend valuable time trying to locate it. If you find that you must often make a quick note when your planner is not at hand, place a notebook or message pad by each telephone in your office for a permanent record. Then transfer the notes, as appropriate. Another neat trick is to purchase a desk pad that has a clear cover to it so you can slip any message under the cover to be acted upon when you are ready.

Once you've established the central planner that you'll use to organize your daily life, it's time to tackle your office. The best time to do this is at the close of business or over the weekend. First, we'll focus on your work surfaces. Remove all the papers and accessories from your desk. Sort the papers into four stacks: active (those papers that you need to do something about), delegate (those papers that you plan to refer to someone else), file (those papers that can be stowed for future reference), and recycle (those papers that can be recycled because you no longer need them). Now create a file folder for these four stacks (don't panic, you won't forget), file the papers, and temporarily set them aside.

Now you can look at all the accessories and toys that used to live on your desk. Now you can say goodbye to all the accessories and toys that used to live on your desk. Your desk surface is your operating table and, like a surgeon's, it should be kept as clean as possible at all times. Each extra object or paper that's on your desk distracts your attention from the matter at hand. One friend of mine is so committed to this that he even has his phone tucked into a drawer. I don't go to that extreme, my phone is on my desk, but I do keep the obligatory stapler, tape dispenser, paper clips, Post-its and pens in a drawer rather than on my desk surface. I've found that keeping the clutter to a minimum frees my mind.

Another consideration about what accessories to keep around your office relates to professional image. Walking into one office, when viewing the desks of the staff, I thought I was visiting a family reunion! Remember office protocol.

Second, take a good long look at your desk drawers, all of them. Does it look as if something is growing there? Or does it look like the corner pharmacy? As with the desk surface, you're going to empty all your drawers— only do it one at a time to keep this process manageable. As you empty the drawers, throw away or set aside those things that do not need to be at your arm's reach all day long. The point of your desk drawers is to keep the tools of your trade close at hand; however, if you keep too much stuff in those drawers, you'll end up losing precious time rooting around for what you really need.

Now you can move along to your file drawers. You need to consider the file drawers at your desk as prime real estate. Only keep in these desk drawer files those papers that you need to consult on a daily basis; all other files should be kept in a filing area outside your office (if they're files you'll need to look at a few times a year) or in a basement long-term retention area (if you need them for your records only).

Facing the fact that you might have too many folders, too many files, and too many types of files may be difficult. Look around, what do you see in your office? Do you see vertical files, horizontal files, and stackable files, plus in and out boxes? Color-coded files are fine, all the red files relate to Project A, while all the D files are personal business, if they relate to pertinent subjects and are not too numerous to ultimately become confusing. Again, the idea is to create a streamlined system that works for your rather than against you.

Take your time deciding which files need to remain in your office, and try to keep the number to a minimum. Office paperwork seems to multiply, and without a clearly defined system that you adhere to, papers will invariably accumulate and you will begin to lose time, files, and patience without a defined system to locate what you are seeking when you need it. Make a decision: If something does not have a specific purpose or function, remove it and store it elsewhere.

Now that you've got your files pared down, it's time to go back to those four new files you created: active, delegate, file, and trash. These four file folders should go at the front of your closest desk file drawer. As paper enters your office, sort it into one of these folders and return to the project at hand. At day's end, make sure that you empty the recycling folder, that you transfer the papers for filing to the outside filing room (or file them in your appropriate desk folders), that you've passed along the projects for delegation (and noted in your planner a tickler file to follow up on their completion), and that you don't have any active papers that need immediate attention. In the morning, check your active folder again and schedule the projects' completion in your planner. It's that simple!

Personally, I keep a running master index of all major projects in a notebook, at least one inch to two inches thick. The projects are arranged in chronological order, the last correspondence being the first item in the book This system is also useful when your files begin to gain weight, and it is now time to put them on a diet. Label the notebooks from the outside and you can quickly and easily reference your notebook and all matters relating to a particular topic. I love this system!

Now that you've shown clutter who's boss, it's time to take a look at how you're handling priorities. Do you find that when the end of another working day arrives, your desk is still piled up with matters of priority, each labeled "Important," "Urgent," or "Time Sensitive"? I remember an employee whose favorite phrase seemed to be "There are only so many hours in a day!" There are, so you must use them wisely. Make a decision about what must be handled and when. Be certain that other people's apathy does not become your emergency. Identify your deadlines and then make a schedule as to how you handle them. Have a plan, then work your plan—every day.

Be deliberate in fulfilling a commitment to yourself to complete a quality product. If you are like me, you have discovered a whole pocket of work that still needs to be done. It just built up, perhaps while you were look-ing the other way. You may have decided that you get your best work done at the last minute. Trust me, if it is the last minute, you are not doing your best work. In the heat of the moment, you don't have the luxury of considering the full array of options and selecting the best one for the job. Worse yet, you might take shortcuts, which compromise the integrity of your work. So start early, don't procrastinate. You will find that catch-up is a very hard game to play. When you delay, the chances of getting the assignment completed diminish. Inevitably, you find a reason to just wait.

To handle excess work, try a retreat and schedule it for one person—yourself—by being in the office, but unavailable to anyone all day. A mayor of one major city always called his "retreats" "advances," because so much was accomplished that would otherwise have been left undone. Let your door be your guard, and your answering service your buffer. You can also work from home for a day; without anyone expecting that you will be there, you may be shocked at how much work you get done!

Be certain that you establish your priorities and that they are not established for you. Life is not all work and no enjoyment, relaxation, or play. Your life does not need to be neatly stacked in little boxes, but you do need to have a clue. You need to access what really counts—to you. Is it the next project at the office—remember there will always be another one—that matters most to you, or would you feel rejuvenated if you could use those tickets to the symphony? Do you have any interest in attending the opening night of the ballet? Have you let your tennis game fall into the doldrums, or have you too long delayed that much-desired trip home to visit your parents, and they are less than three hours away?

You need balance to beat burnout. When you feel overwhelmed, the first response is to find reasons that you cannot do anything about it. A friend reminded me that there is something you can do to help the situation no matter what you are doing and where you are in the world, and that is breathe. You have to do it anyway to survive. So slow down and try this exercise. Close your eyes or focus straight ahead, create your own exercise, but concentrate on deep breathing for ten to sixty seconds to find your deepest resolve to press on.

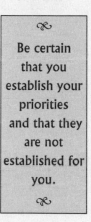

Be certain that you establish your priorities and that they are not established for you.

Don't make the mistake of trying to make life one thing or another. It cannot be separated. It is not either/or. Life is both/and; it is addition, not subtraction. Therefore, envision a scale of justice. You want to make sure that both sides are balanced without that nagging feeling or reality that you are never home to help your children with their homework, take care of the lawn, prepare the meals, go to a favorite movie, or just "chill." You can make certain that outstanding success in one aspect of your life is not an abysmal failure in the another.

Conversely, there are times when you have to make a real decision about what gives you bread and butter. When others want you to "just come on and go or do," you have to look at your requirements and fulfill them. It may mean that you "just don't" do anything with any-body, particularly if you need to become isolated and insulated to get the job done. Since I know that my speeches do not come to me in a dream and that I must research and write them, I become unavail-able, unapologetically. It is called reality.

Another method I have for keeping my life manageable and serene is something I call set-asides. These are moments that I consciously set aside for myself. Some people thrive on receiving a call a minute; I don't. In my opinion, the information society has possibly overaccessed us with e-mails, pagers, and telephones and cellular phones.

> ⚭
>
> It is not either/or. Life is both/and; it is addition, not subtraction.
>
> ⚭

Whether you gravitate toward or away from the constant access, just remember, whatever your choice, that you are the only you that you have for your-self. Give yourself some breathing room. There are times when you may need to turn your access off and proceed with what you are doing, uninterrupted.

Think of the times you have picked up the telephone and people just start in nonstop for the next thirty min-utes or more. They are totally oblivious to what you are doing. Their concern is that they want to talk with you. You may need to kindly convey to them that you are "in a meeting," "just walking out the door," "would be glad to let them speak with your office assistant to arrange an appointment for another telephone appointment"—anything! When I am the caller, I typically begin the call by asking, "Is this a good time?" My inquiry seems to always be appreciated. Face it. There are periods during the workday when another time would just be better. Why not try establishing a particular part of your day to return phone messages as well as your e-mails? Otherwise, it may be more than slightly disruptive to take every incoming call or message. But I do urge you to return your calls. It is necessary, because you cannot predict what is important and what is not.

When in a supervisory role, initially I held steadfast to an open-door policy. I wanted all my staff to know that any time they wanted to talk they could do so. Wrong! I ran into people who wanted to chat ad infinitum about issues that would have best been handled by their first-line supervisor or, conversely, who wanted to engage in small talk. Either way, time was not only consumed, but swallowed. To solve the concern and still allow access, I designated hours on a specific day to talk with the staff, and it worked much better for me.

People who still insist on "just dropping by" can be given a hint, unless they are from another world, that you really don't have the time or inclination to chat if you keep standing when they come into your office. Probably, they will tire and move on.

I've also come across some other tricks for saving time in my day. The first trick is to avoid bottlenecks. If you already know to expect a traffic jam during the rush hour, a long lunch line at the deli, or an incessant busy signal on the Internet, work around it by planning your time, by altering your hours for arrival and departure, your lunchtime, or when you take a ride on the communication highway. Try to use the Internet when the access is more immediate, although I am not positive just when that would be. The best time to do your banking is probably not Friday afternoon at four P.M. It is logical to assume that at least half the city will have the same idea!

Schedule and attend meetings only when they are necessary. Too often I have gotten the strange feeling that people enjoy meeting just for the sake of meeting! There should always be an agenda, a true purpose to the meeting, and some substantive information shared, and most likely there will also be some action items. Many meetings can be handled, I have found, by a telephone conversation or by someone else serving as your representative.

Think carefully when you are making an appointment. I view it as a commitment. When you interact with others, respect is soon gained for people who make appointments and keep them. If the appointment seems unimportant or unnecessary, then don't lead a person on by making it in the first place. The good reputation that you have or are seeking to build is all that you really have, so don't blow it by being careless or inconsiderate. Time is money.

At one time there was a power lunch, which has now become a quick, healthy power breakfast. Those who can see their desk in their dreams are trying to get to the office, not spend more time outside it. Some have resorted to a very timely early morning meeting at their office for coffee or tea. It works very well, and the commodity of time is saved. While meeting with a foundation director, I flew in for the breakfast meeting that was held in her conference room. All participants were in the building and just came up for the meeting. Not a minute was wasted on travel time. Better yet, it was a fruitful meeting: our grant was approved. Have breakfast or lunch in the office and have a meeting around it. There are forty-nine working weeks a year, and if you subtract the holidays, 225 midday opportunities remain.

When you are planning a program, do the audience and yourself a huge favor; prepare a specific, not generic, script for every program participant. They will know exactly how many minutes they have to make their remarks. At one event, the speaker decided that he wanted to further expound on his point, about which he was very passionate, but the program planner rushed to the stage and explained, "Not tonight, you won't!" The audience was truly tickled and relieved. It was at this event that I witnessed a three-hour program, nonfood function that had a standing-room-only attendance, which still kept everyone captivated because of the excellent organization of the program. It is sage advice: "If you fail to plan, you can plan to fail!"

A speechwriter shares the story of always carrying a single-edge razor blade with him so that when he reads a newspaper or a magazine he can quickly cut out an article that pertains to a certain topic.

Once you have started the process of getting yourself more organized and have become more committed to being present for that which is important and realizing that you really are just one person, you must work hard to maintain your achievement. Be encouraged. As you organize, many new, exciting, and helpful techniques will slip into your knowledge reservoir. At first you may be apprehensive about seeing a clear picture of yourself in your organized office and feeling that you are actually productive, without being stressed out. The picture may be fuzzy at first, but at the end you will be able to see much more clearly, like a fresh and welcome warm spring day. Endeavor!

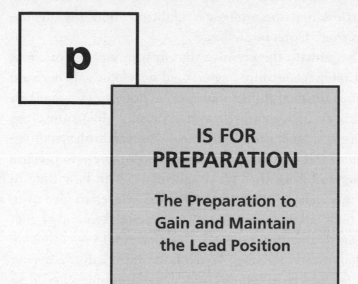

p

IS FOR PREPARATION

The Preparation to Gain and Maintain the Lead Position

Alot of work goes into winning. Before the sprinter takes his victory lap, the architect accepts the award, the actress acknowledges her standing ovation, or the sales representative gets the big bonus, there come hours, days, weeks, years, and even decades of preparation. The sprinter adheres to a grueling daily regimen of diet and training, the architect goes through years of schooling and then humbly apprentices under a seasoned mentor, the actress submits to scores of auditions and, like the sales representative, most often hears rejection. And after all that, in their moment of glory, their performance often will look so elegant, polished, and effortless that the audience might presume they hadn't even tried. Don't be fooled.

Begin with the premise that in your coursework, job, charitable leadership, or personal development there are some additional things that can be done to give you real assurance and comfort for the future. Most often, the future is shaped not by outwardly imposed rules and regulations that box us in, but by our willingness to prepare ourselves for all that life might offer. The best time to begin is today. To be sure, it is often easier to give in to the temptation to live for the moment. Remember that the satisfaction that comes with quick indulgence, though, is shallow and fleeting. Try to find and relish the deeper gratification that comes from denying momentary pleasures in favor of dedicating yourself to a disciplined daily practice. In addition to honing your talent, your constant commitment to preparing yourself for a better tomorrow will energize your sense of purpose and enrich your self-concept. Self-esteem comes from doing estimable things, and developing your gifts is most definitely commendatory. When you have done quality work, when you have given something your best shot, you will not need to be applauded, your heart will know and tell you so. Close your eyes and visualize the possibilities your preparation will make manifest and start walking in that direction.

If you ever visit New York and ask how to get to Carnegie Hall, you are most likely to be told: "Practice, practice, practice." From today forward, remember that regardless of where you want to go in life, the same answer applies: "Practice, practice, practice." Even if you've chosen a vocation or avocation that comes naturally to you, you'll be that much further ahead if you put some effort and preparation behind your talent.

Prepare and stay on your toes because every day, in large or small ways, you have the opportunity to show up for yourself and the world. It's a privilege! So many times, we miss out on the main show; when the long-awaited day arrives, we are absent, because we have majored in the minor. My friend Fran will never forget the day she blew a big promotion that her manager worked hard to line up for her because she wasn't prepared and she failed to show up. On the appointed morning, her boss had been bragging to her superiors about what a resourceful, reliable, and dynamic sales representative Fran was and how she'd make a great regional manager. They waited and waited to secretly observe Fran in action at a sales training session, only Fran never appeared because she decided that it was more important to pack her bags for her departure than to attend the first meeting of the day. She picked the wrong day to skip school! And actually there never is a good day and rarely a good reason to skip a scheduled activity. If it's on your agenda, be there.

Here are other ways that we major in the minor (or lose the forest for the trees): We decide to postpone indefinitely getting in touch with prospective clients because we can't afford a slick marketing piece to introduce our services; we sit out an important industry event even because we don't have a suit that looks sharp enough; we miss our moment in the sun because we forget out lines; or we arrive half an hour late for a job interview and find our appointment canceled. Preparation is like having a first-aid kit and knowing exactly where it is and how to use it. It helps you avoid being in a jam. Prepare.

Sometimes some of us think that we think we can bluff our way to success. Rather than prepare, we assume an air of entitlement, thinking our prospective clients will believe that we are qualified, certified, or authorized, when in actuality we are not. We only succeed in fooling ourselves. Complacency, arrogance, and lethargy ultimately undercut performance. Either separately or together, they will crack a weak foundation, expose a pseudo persona, put you on a collision course on your make-believe expressway, and cancel your audition for the main character in *To Be*. When you think you're good enough to wing it or tomorrow is soon enough to prepare, listen for the wake-up call. It will come. Preparation, like the law, is a jealous mistress, and she must be courted.

> ❧
>
> Preparation is like having a first-aid kit and knowing exactly where it is and how to use it. It helps you avoid being in a jam.
>
> ❧

If opportunity keeps passing you by, maybe it's because you aren't ready for it. When something doesn't go my way, my first step is to take a long hard look in the mirror. Rather than blame my misfortune on injustice or bum luck, it's far more constructive to figure out that if opportunity keeps passing me by, maybe it's because I'm not prepared. I must consider honestly the role I played and whether I played it to the hilt or halfheartedly. Then I look myself in the eyes and I resolve to become fully prepared to fulfill the part, without ambivalence.

Avoid the inevitable; prepare. Look back over your life and consider those periods when your level of preparation was lacking. The market report was returned because it was vague and skipped important details. Or there was no buy-in to the new project you proposed because you didn't take time to think through and describe its benefits. Or, my personal nightmare, my speech is greeted with lukewarm applause because I didn't take adequate time to tailor my message to the specific audience. It feels like I might as well have been talking to an open field, because I skipped the research to locate the relevant facts and anecdotes that would connect to my audience. Because I opted to play rather than fully prepare, my audience was lost or wished it had been. That is not an experience I plan ever to repeat, and armed with adequate preparation, I need not live it again.

Studying for the test creates a reasonable expectation for success after completing the examination. Before the fact, we have the responsibility to review our notes, all outside lectures and reference books. We must be thorough, not casual or overly convinced that the coursework is easy and we have it all down to a science. Inevitably, the student who tries to convince me that "there is no need to study," and "I know exactly what the questions will be" ends up with a "C" or "B" grade. False confidence gives false predictions.

During my preparation for a major exam in law

school, I decided that I was exhausted and it was time to turn in; I walked to the window and looked out over the campus and could see any number of lights still burning! I quickly reassessed my decision, realized I wasn't that tired, and decided to press on. Those other students would possibly be taking the same exam and competing for the same "A" (we were graded on a curve). If they could prepare by burning the midnight oil, so could I!

Whether in school or in the workplace, let's put some starch in our curriculum courses or on-the-job training choices. To make selections that merely fulfill the graduation requirements or that give you just enough training to meet your job requirements without more will not take you to the winner's circle. Sign up for opportunities that will stretch you, that will force you to paddle harder. You can do it; the only question is whether you will do it. The answer depends on you.

What obstacle has ever kept you from hitting the mark? Is it related to your basic education or additional training for the job? Is it your own insistence that you are just too busy to stop and prepare for what you know you need to do? Is it procrastination to keep up with the latest technology? Trust me, these chinks in your preparation will grow into respectable chasms, even as you seek to ignore them, rationalize them, or place them on a figurative back burner. They can take on their own life and grow. Eventually, there are no sunglasses dark enough to block them out, no adequate explanation to excuse them, and no back burner upon which to place them. Sooner or later, you will have to prepare yourself for the present and future realities, or prepare yourself to finish dead last.

What can each of us do now to make sure that we're ready to embrace every opportunity that comes our way? U.S. Secretary of Labor Robert Reich recently offered this recipe for success in the new economy of the twenty-first century:

> "Become computer literate, regardless of the type of work you do.
> Education will give you an edge, but you must continuously build new knowledge and skills.
> Don't think of your career in a linear way. Plan on advancing because of skills, not seniority.
> Be aggressive about networking. Information is the key to advancement."

There is no "I" in team, People will work in teams, though team means may be dispersed and connected by technology. Enhance your value by learning to play all the positions.

Clearly, complacency is not a winning attribute. You can be prepared or be left behind, but nothing and nobody will stand still while you make up your mind.

Tough assignments do not require timid preparation. While the global community is bilingual, many Americans are still insisting that they speak English, first, only, and always. English is fundamental; however, additional language proficiencies are greatly desired. Remember that speaking only one language, while so many people around the world speak two or more, is curable. Get on your case.

Learn a second language, and you'll find that many more doors are open to you.

Hold fast to a standard of excellence; otherwise, you will be dwarfed by the competition. Microsoft's Bill Gates, with a fortune of $20 billion says, "You always have to be thinking about who's coming to get you." In the real world you are only as good as your last success story. You can believe your own press clippings if you like and devastation may be waiting around the corner. You must be prepared to prove yourself every time. If you compare this reality to a play, each presentation is act one; to a song, each verse the first; to a book, the first chapter. You must face the fact the supporters or competitors alike question whether you can "pull it off" one more time, and then one more time.

> ❧
> You must be prepared to prove yourself every time. If you compare this reality to a play, each presentation is act one; to a song, each verse the first; to a book, the first chapter.
> ❧

Your responsibility is not to go on automatic pilot. When you have the top slot you have to work to get it and to keep it, because everyone else wants to take your place. You must possess the winning combination of preparation, knowledge, training, or skill, and a will or drive to get the job done. To that end, you also must knock indifference out of your consciousness. Research shows that those who actually do their work on the job and reduce the time spent on personal calls or complaining by just one half-hour a day (four extra days per year) were better prepared to actually deal with their work assignment.

The world is waiting for more people who are prepared unequivocally to meet the challenges life presents. We need people who know more, who can engage in critical thinking, who can disagree without being disagreeable, who can take creative initiative, who can separate sense from nonsense, who can anticipate and adjust to change, and who can see the connection between seemingly unrelated events. We need people who are prepared to lead with their strengths. Prepare to lead!

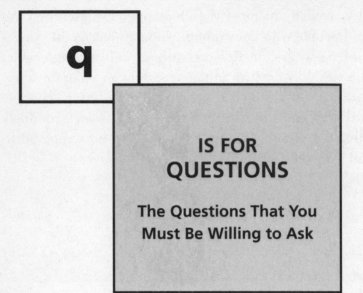

q

IS FOR QUESTIONS

The Questions That You Must Be Willing to Ask

When we were children, the word *why?* was our favorite refrain. "Why does it get dark?" "Why do we have to wear shoes?" "Why do the leaves fall down?" "Why does the cat purr?" At a young age, we were intent on pressing and learning and absorbing as much as possible. We accepted little at face value. Our need to know usurped any concern over appearances. Unfortunately, with each passing year, we allowed our egos and fears to silence our native inquisitiveness. We learned less, assumed more, grew stagnant. Why?

Questions shine bright, lights illuminate closed and

sometimes locked drawers, doors, or memories. Questions can lead to discomfort today but, on the other side, they can lead to a better tomorrow. It's important to take off the rose-colored glasses with respect to all aspects of your life and to begin to ask, "Why?"

Have you stopped recently to ask yourself why you are in your chosen profession? Work is the place where we spend the largest percentage of our active lifetime, and it's important to make sure that we are investing that time for conscious reasons. Sometimes the reason that someone entered a career five years or ten years prior becomes obsolete or less significant. Let's say that you became an outside sales representative because you were convinced that it would allow you to rise or fall on the strength of your own sales ability. Then too you liked the freedom it gave you to work when and where you chose. Perhaps, ten years into the job, you still enjoy selling but you realize that you'd like to find a position that involves less travel and a steadier paycheck and that would allow you to put down roots and begin a family. The growing gap between your personal and professional goals could be the reason you feel so dissatisfied with your work and reluctant to make the next sales call.

> ❧
> **Have you stopped recently to ask yourself why?**
> ❧

Career management can be complicated, because when you paint yourself into a corner there is no room to breathe. If you are determined to enjoy life, raise your family, participate in community and church activities, be a true-blue friend, and excel in your career, you may find that your ambitious intentions overwhelm your ability to fulfill them. You'll need to have the courage and tenacity to listen to your inner voice and consider what matters to you most, often irrespective of what others tell you should matter to you. And you'll need to get honest with yourself about what you can and cannot accomplish in this lifetime.

In my own experience, my honest questioning of the relationship between my personal and professional goals led to a major change in my career path. It wasn't easy. There I was; after years of academic training and professional experience, I'd landed a secure, prestigious government job. But, after ten years of legal practice, I wanted to spread my wings professionally, and I yearned for work that would give me enough time to enjoy the love of my life. The contemplation was professional and personal; both decisions were major. Change brings about a change. I had decided to marry, to relocate with my new husband to San Antonio, Texas, and to become an entrepreneur—all in one fell swoop. In some ways, professionally, I felt relieved as a senior manager that I could now lay my burden down. After the wedding vows, I began the real journey with my always friend, stalwart companion, and very significant other.

It's also critical to take an honest look at your closest relationships. At one point in her life, one woman realized that she'd surrounded herself with very needy people. As a result of her own insecurity, perhaps, this person only felt she was worthy of a friend if she could give that person something he or she needed. She didn't stop to look at what she could receive from that person in terms of companionship, support, guidance, or otherwise. As a result, when she faced a personal crisis in her own life, she found herself in the company of a lot of self-involved people who could not be there for her.

Take a look at the relationships in your life. Ask yourself "why?" in terms of the company you keep. Do you enjoy and value these relationships? When you spend time with them, do you feel elevated by the experience? Do they inspire you to reach for your dreams and to lead a better life? Do you look forward to spending time in their presence? As you make these evaluations, keep in mind that healthy relationships are full of give and take. Also, remember that each and every relationship is a choice.

There are some people in my life who in large and small ways, knowingly and unknowingly, have shaped my life. They have helped me to halt my troublesome ways, to turn the other cheek and walk away, to plan, to refrain from overreacting, and to become a person of second chances. They have been there when I have missed a goal, been anxious, or celebrated.

Now take a moment to make an inventory of the top ten issues that concern you. These issues can involve your personal or professional life, your community, or society. Make a chart with three columns: one for the problems, one for the instigator, and one for a corrective action. Within each column, take care to answer the inherent questions associated with each. For instance, in the problem column, you'll need to name the problem and describe why it's a problem. In the next column, you'll need to note why it happened and who or what was responsible. The goal of this inventory, as with any inventory, is to ask the questions and uncover the facts so you can get a clear, honest understanding of the issues that trouble you and then find the appropriate responses toward resolving those issues. Take care, particularly with column two, that you don't find yourself consistently pointing the finger of blame elsewhere. Remember the wisdom in the popular saying, "There are no victims, only volunteers."

In 1980, I gave a speech inspired by Winston Churchill's questions: "If Not You, Who? If Not Now, When?" Those questions have helped to catapult others and myself into a conviction that the responsibility for change begins at our feet. So the next time I noticed any social ill—the erosion of our public education system, the growing pollution of the American landscape, the rise in violent crime and urban decay, the increased polarization of the races, economic barriers to proper health care, and more—I had to ask myself, "What can I do to advance a positive solution to this problem?" No longer could I be content to talk around a salient issue or stand on the sidelines.

If you were raised to avoid uncomfortable questions, to go with the flow, to acquiesce, you need to make a paradigm shift. You must begin to question and acknowledge the considerable influence you can exert to alter or break systems, attitudes, rules, and behaviors that run counter to your core values. You must again give voice to your childlike impulse to ask, "Why?" about all that you don't understand or accept. You must abandon your seat in the silent symphony.

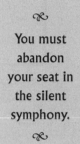

You must abandon your seat in the silent symphony.

Be prepared: One question will lead to another, and it's impossible to know where any of them lead. Strengthen your resolve with the knowledge that positive change relies heavily, if not singularly, on those who are willing to ask the questions, get the answers, and take the necessary action. The examined life is not a comfortable, easy life but it is the only life worth living.

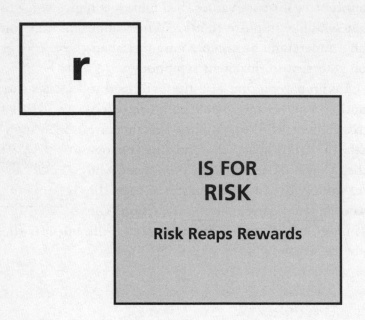

r

IS FOR
RISK

Risk Reaps Rewards

Sometimes the wrong question keeps us from taking the first step. How often have you considered a new activity and then dismissed it after asking yourself, "What if I fail?" What would have happened if you'd asked yourself, "What if I succeed?" Would you have done it? Think back to how the scales tip when you weigh all your life's successes against your failures. Looks to me like it's a better bet to take the risk that you'll succeed.

After years of recruiting and managing employees on the basis of how well they could toe the line and avoid mistakes, corporate America finally has begun to clamor for "risk takers." Management has awakened to the fact that fast and significant advances ride on the backs of those who have the vision and courage to take a risk and venture into a completely new area. It also has realized that allowing each worker to have more free rein, to take a risk, resulted in tapping more of that employee's ingenuity and creativity for the company's benefit. Now, an employment record dotted with some failures looks better than a spotless one: It's assumed that the latter is the track record of one who hasn't taken enough risks that could lead his team to big rewards.

Make risk your partner in business and in life, but don't make it a silent one. You must get acquainted with it and keep it in the forefront of your thinking and actions. It will enhance ever aspect of your life; it will allow your spirit to soar. As General Patton said: "The whole joy of life is taking chances, to build enough faith to destroy all our fears."

> ❧
> It will enhance every aspect of your life; it will allow your spirit to soar.
> ❧

The reality is that risk taking is becoming mandatory. As the Internet and other technological advances weave the world together more tightly, fresh ideas and approaches travel around the world at the speed of light, influencing those it leaves in its wake. If you are hemmed in to your old routine, if you continue to stick with what has worked for you in the past, you will become stagnant and fall behind. You must continue to seek out new and different approaches to your daily life. In short, you must venture in order to gain.

Risk is not for the faint of heart. It requires a tremendous amount of courage, tenacity, and faith to move outside your comfort zone. Once you take the first step, you don't know where the next one will lead. All you know is that you have set in motion an entirely new chain of events, and it will take all your know-how to handle the unexpected opportunities and challenges that await you. Take heart: the rewards are bountiful.

What is your appetite for risk? Here's a quick self-diagnostic test so that you can see where you stand on the risk-taking continuum.

Risk Threshold Survey

Name: _____ Date: _____

Directions: Circle the response next to each statement that best describes you.

1. When going out to eat, I prefer to try out a new restaurant.

Always   Sometimes   Never

2. I enjoy going to parties and meeting new people.

Always   Sometimes   Never

3. When a new consumer electronic product hits the market (e.g., CD players, palm-sized computers), I'm the first within my circle of friends to buy it.

Always   Sometimes   Never

4. When I see someone at a business meeting that I don't recognize, I'm the first one to reach out my hand and introduce myself.

Always   Sometimes   Never

5. In sporting activities, whether hiking or sailing or running, I like to go farther and faster than anyone else.

Always   Sometimes   Never

6. When another team member proposes a sweeping initiative that sounds extremely positive, I'm most likely to jump on board and pledge my full support.

Always   Sometimes   Never

7. When my child asks me if he can go on a school trip overseas and it fits within the family budget, I lend him my enthusiastic support and suggest that he contribute to his spending money for the trip by taking on an extra job.

Always   Sometimes   Never

8. I like to find new and different ways of tackling the same old thing.

Always   Sometimes   Never

9. I find change exciting and refreshing.

Always   Sometimes   Never

10. I have faith that the risks I take will pay off richly.

Always   Sometimes   Never

If you answered "always" to each question, congratulations, you have a high tolerance for risk and you are well suited to thrive in today's entrepreneurial environment. If you answered "sometimes" to five or more questions, you are somewhat risk-adverse and might consider increasing your appetite slowly but surely. For instance, once a week, consider making no plans for your leisure time, and on the appointed day, select something completely new to try out. If, on the other hand, you answered "never" to five or more questions, you are already taking the biggest risk of all: the risk that the rest of the world is going to pass you by. In your case, the next time you start to shake your head no, stop and question the motive behind your resistance. If it's fear-based, then stop shaking no and start nodding yes. Watch those around you who make bolder moves. How do they talk to themselves? What do they say that convinces them to take the plunge while you're still just testing the waters? Remember, each time you do something that feels scary and different and risky, you gain experience that emboldens you to do it for a second and third time and perhaps more.

One clue that you're not taking enough risks is that you feel as if your life is in a rut. If you're feeling that way, now's a great time to break the self-imposed lock on rigid thinking and preconceived ideas that there is no other way to approach problems, situations, or people. Don't allow your fear to continue to corral your natural avant-garde impulses, to clip your creativity, to keep you in a lock-step adherence to everyday sameness. One word describes the result, *boring*, and in business, the one word is even harsher, it is *defeat*. Break free from your rut now!

When I take a risk, I feel really alive. When I craft a new speech, I like to do something that will wake up my audience at the beginning, middle, and end. Often, I employ the technique of a scat singer and use my voice to imitate an instrument or a mechanism. In one of my speeches, "The Wakeup Call," I decided to punctuate the speech with a loud "Brrrrrrrrrrrrrrrrrrrrrrring!" that sounds like an old-fashioned wind-up alarm clock. At the time I made this decision, I realized that I was taking a risk, that the audience might respond with shocked silence or a straight-jacket. But my gut said, "Go, girl," and I did. And the moment my voice filled the hall with the first "Brrrrrrrrrrrrring!" I felt my spirit soar on the joyous flight of the unknown. It was exciting, exhilarating, outrageous, and I was completely alive. It made me realize that taking risks not only takes me to a new dimension, it also helps to keep me young at heart!

> ⤬
> When I take a risk, I feel really alive.
> ⤬

Top performers understand the need to make exceptions to the rule; to brainstorm for a fresh idea, and to step outside the established boundary of "This is the way we do things around here." Most often they are not well-liked by their counterparts, who'd prefer to reside in the false security of the routine, and yet their intuition calls so strongly in favor of progress that they won't allow themselves to be held back by the herd instincts. They innately understand the wisdom in this piece of contrary advice from business leaders Robert J. Kriegel and Louis Patleer: "The biggest risk is not to risk."

Most often, when I find myself afraid to try something new, it's because I'm afraid of losing something that I have or of not getting something that I want. If what I have is far more valuable than what I'll gain by taking the risk, then it's a healthy fear. On the other hand, and frankly this is the most typical scenario, if what I'm afraid of losing is something with little or no meaning to me, then I need to let go and move forward. For example, let's look at those times that I've been afraid to start a workout program at a gym because I don't like the shape I'm in. Now, clearly, what I'm afraid of losing (i.e., other peoples' image of me fully clothed, I suppose) is not more valuable than my health and fitness. Plus, examined in the cold light of day, I can laugh at myself in this example and realize that I am not about to become the center of attention at the gym. Each person there will be busier attending to his or her own physique than checking me out.

When you get right down to it, it is pretty simple; you have to play the game to win. If you play with the cards so close to your chest, never looking beyond the past and your comfort in the present, you will miss out on bigger rewards in the future. Plus, since life is a game of chance, let's look at the odds. If past performance is a good indicator, the odds are that every try that you make is not going to be a failure, especially if you keep trying. Your success depends on thinking quickly and thinking smart and thinking ahead. You may think that it is senseless to go out onto uncharted water, but it is senseless not to. Just where do you think your competition is setting their sights and sails? If you don't want to find your-self waving in their tailwind, you must do the same.

To get ahead or even to stay even, you must dare to bring your heart, mind, and soul to the task of venturing beyond the status quo. You'll have to dare to dig deep, and still deeper, to call forth all your assets. You'll have to dare to join the party and bring something to the table. You'll have to dare your fear of failure and realize that nothing beats a failure but a try.

Life is a risk, but we live it. Every day is a leap of faith. Jump high!

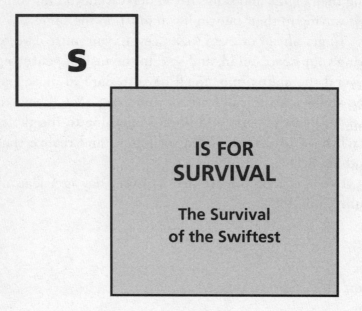

S

IS FOR
SURVIVAL

The Survival
of the Swiftest

Every new advancement in technology brings with it a new set of conveniences and expectations. When we went from telegraphs to telephone, it was anticipated that we would communicate more frequently with our correspondents. When we moved to calculators from the slide rule, it was expected that we would perform more calculations in less time and with greater accuracy. When we abandoned "snail mail" for faxes, overnight packages, and e-mail, it was expected that we'd pick up our pace and speed our response time. Progress breeds still more progress. Those who resist its forward movement, those who refuse to progress alongside, will not survive.

Life is an escalator: You can move forward or backward; you can not remain still. To move ahead, you will need to keep all your survival tools sharp. In our changing world, you will need to hone continuously your communication skills (verbal and written), your ability to lead others, your willingness to learn, your flexibility and openness to new approaches, your technological savvy, your financial acumen, and your community commitment. You must stay on your toes!

The workplace has changed radically with the emergence of a globally interdependent marketplace and a technologically interconnected workforce. The traditional fixed five-year planning cycle has been abandoned for three-year, one-year, and six-month plans in turn. Each day, workers and managers must be prepared for a new wave of retooling and reengineering designed to keep their employer ahead of the curve and certain extinction. In this environment of constant flux, the rewards flow to the low-maintenance workers, the so-called self-starters who don't sit static waiting for a cue that may never be given. A quotation from the United Technologies employee

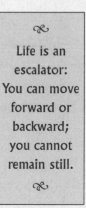

ᔟ
Life is an escalator: You can move forward or backward; you cannot remain still.
ᔟ

manual comes to mind: "If you want to manage somebody; manage yourself. Do that well and you'll be ready to stop managing and start leading."

Across the nation, there's an exciting trend of non-traditional, older students enrolling in higher education. In some cases, I have seen parents and their children matriculating on the same college campus and taking the same courses. One of my corporate clients has a requirement that every person in its employ must take ten hours of advanced academic training at the company's expense and time. This client recognizes that education is the catalyst in the twenty-first century.

In addition to knowledge, economics will play a role in your survival. Most employers have long since abandoned the responsibility to design a pension that will provide for you in your retirement. The quality of your life before and after your retirement now lies squarely in your hands. Treat your salary with respect. Take the first portion of each week's pay and place it into an account or fund that will grow future earnings. Also keep a prudent reserve liquid in the event of a "rainy day." Build your knowledge of sound business and investment practices and opportunities through regular reading of the financial section of the newspaper. Consider joining an investment club. And protect your family's future with insurance, wills, and estate planning. Start now.

Develop life-sustaining and enriching relationships. You never know where you might find them. I agreed to join the board of directors for an organization because I believed in its professed mission. At the first board meeting, I was delighted to find myself in the presence of a group of people who were not only committed to the same organization, but who also were highly competent and caring. We all really got to know one another and our families and our individual and shared challenges and bliss. Because we truly cared for one another—at the human level—we worked superlatively as a unit, leaving none of the organization's work undone or half-done.

It's important to surround yourself with positive and supportive relationships because there are many unhappy and unhealthy individuals who will try to make you their company. (We all know what misery loves!) The very hard, cold reality is that these people are, for whatever reason, jealous, self-interested, insincere, and dishonest, and they will try mightily to diminish your worth and accomplishments. Spending too much time in their presence can erode your self-confidence and throw you off course. When you find yourself so surrounded, when you sense a climate of intimidation, puffery, and pretense, take solace in these words from Theodore Roosevelt:

> It is not the critic who counts, not the man who points out how the strong man stumbles or where the doer of deeds could have done better. The credit belongs to the man who is actually in the arena, whose face is marred by dust and sweat and gloom, who strives valiantly, who errs and comes up short again and again because there is no effort without error and shortcomings, who knows the great devotion, who spends himself in a worthy cause, who at best knows in the end the high achievement of triumph and who at worst, if he fails while daring greatly, knows his place shall

never be with those timid and cold souls who know neither victory nor defeat.

And, at the first opportunity, make tracks. You cannot change those who wish it not. Instead, as my friend David Shea advises "Let go, move on, go lightly."

On your journey through the adventures of the twenty-first century, make sure that you have these tools in your survival belt:

- **Preparation:** Keep your physical and mental antenna tuned and high so that you are ready for whatever life brings. Rather than cringing when receiving news or notice of a forthcoming change or innovation, anticipate the skills it will require and embrace the learning opportunities inherent in their acquisition. Then suit up and show up: You are up to the task.

- **Awareness:** Practice seeing your environment— at home, at work, and elsewhere—for how it is rather than how you'd like it to be. Denial is a slippery space and far more treacherous than reality. Always make sure that you know who is on your side and who is at your side. Try to uncover the true source of any friction and resolve it. Spend more time posing questions than making assumptions.

- **Flexibility:** Do you spend a lot of time finding fault and criticizing rather than adjusting yourself to the circumstances? If you remain rigid, the

winds of change will snap you in two. Practice
flexibility in your daily life. Try switching
long-held routines to keep yourself fresh and
open to fluctuation. The more adroit you become
at accepting and handling voluntary
change, the better prepared you'll be
to field life's little curve balls.

- **Packaging:** Right or wrong, your
movement up the career, social, and
civic ladders will be propelled in part
by your presentation. Your grooming,
manner of speech, style of dress,
and social graces create the first
impression that others receive and
often retain forever. Make sure your "outside"
accurately reflects all the promise that your
"inside" brings to any table.

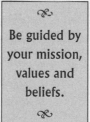

If you remain
rigid, the
winds of
change will
snap you in
two.

- **Selectivity:** You cannot and will not be all things
to all people. Learn to say no. Otherwise, you will
find that you are trying to do too much and nothing is being done to satisfaction. Let
your daily affairs and choices be
guided by your mission, values, and
beliefs. Make sure that the tasks you
list on your "to do" pass muster with
your core truths, order them by priority, and see each one through from
start to finish. Be prepared for other people's
attempts to slip a "must do!" on your plate (you

Be guided by
your mission,
values and
beliefs.

know the type who allow their apathy and disor-
ganization to create your emergency!) and keep
their urgency in perspective. Be certain that you
are not doing more than you can do well; quality
is what you seek, not quantity.

• **Fortitude:** Life is a game of hardball and the
bases are loaded. Those who stay in the game will
have to endure the strikes, the fouls, and the fast
pitch until life's umpire calls, "You're out!" Those
who really learn how to play the game deal with it
when somebody new comes along and moves all
the bases! If you are fragile, you will give in and
give out. You will become demoralized, distracted,
or derailed by the antics of others. Learn to hang
tough and allow the harsh words of others to roll
right off. Take consolation from the African
proverb: "It is not what you call me, it is what I
answer to!" Then exert some energy, pull up until
you are standing mentally, emotionally, and
spiritually, and move forward.

• **Distinction:** Spend more time trying to find your
own true voice and less time trying to tune it to
please others. In my life, I have never sought to
be similar to or the same as anyone else. I am
grateful for every distinction and nuance that
gives me my own singular identity. In my
achievements, I seek to make a personal imprint,
to leave an impression that says unmistakably
presented and prepared by yours truly. I have

been self-assured without seeking to assuage anyone's ego or my own. Find your own voice and
sing out: It will add to the harmony.

- **Expectant:** Live life with an expectant spirit.
  Believe in the worth of all creation, anticipate
  that it will bear fruit, and it will in its own time
  and way. News flash! If you set the goal at
  nothing, it is for sure that you will hit it every
  time. We all rise to meet the expectation—ours
  and others. Let's keep the bar raised high!

- **Perseverance:** Whatever the reason, withdrawal
  is concession and an admission that you can't.
  Remaining steadfast is more than half of the task
  to which you are more than equal. The time and
  place of your surrender will be the chapter in
  your personal history that will cause you regret.
  Remain when others abandon. Stand firm.
  Expect others to challenge your views, listen to
  their objections, but don't retreat.

- **Community:** If you do not already have a
  supportive community of friends, advisers, and
  mentors you trust, begin today to form this inner
  circle. Seek out people with whom you can share
  openly and speak freely, and from whom you can
  gain information and insight. (My beloved
  mentor, when speaking of my willingness to reach
  out, says, "If she does not know then she will
  ask!") The ability to ask for help, especially in our
  fast-moving and complex world, often has

determined the quality and longevity of a life. Plus, your physical, mental, and emotional health will benefit when you share your voice with others, bounce around ideas and concepts, and engage in lively and thought-provoking sessions. Remember: "United you stand . . ."

Each of these qualities will allow you to survive and thrive. Take heart if your quotient of some is lower than others. Work toward developing those skills that are less pronounced. Like all human beings, you are a work in progress. Take heart. The first and most important step to survival begins every morning.

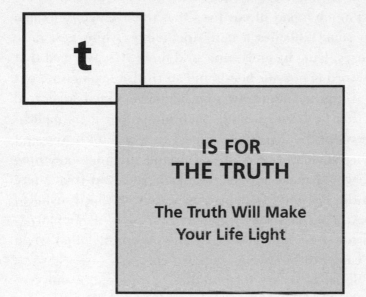

t

IS FOR
THE TRUTH

The Truth Will Make
Your Life Light

"The truth, the whole truth, and nothing but the truth, so help me, God," is a pledge we might consider making each day, rather on those rare occasions when we have to testify in court. For each day that you choose instead to go for the quick fix, to compromise your integrity, and to make bargain-basement agreements, you pull down the shades on your life. Witness those whose lives are shrouded in shady deals and notice what their walk eventually attracts. Truth requires more attention to devotion than duty. At the end of the day it is yourself with whom you must live.

According to psychologist Dr. Joyce Brothers, "Lying is so much a part of our lives that the average American tells some 200 lies a day," including "white lies, false excuses, lying by omission," and more. It's assumed that our word is not our bond, and so truth seekers tune out our words and study our body language. One banker told me that he'd denied more than one major loan application when the applicant refused to look him in the eye. He assumed the person was trying to hide something and would make a poor financial risk. And then there was the fast-food franchisee who told me he'd installed an extra set of security cameras to track his employees and to deter their pilferage. The deterrent failed when the cameras themselves were stolen!

Some of us try to minimize or rationalize our tendency to be less than forthright. Women believe that it's acceptable, even de rigueur, to lie about their age. (One judge asks witnesses to state their age before being sworn in so they wouldn't instantly perjure themselves.) We try to convince ourselves and others that we only "bend the truth" when it's necessary to protect the feelings or welfare of another. Please! If our willingness to lie was ever in fact necessary, we seem to have taken it to the extreme, all the way to the smallest daily interaction with another person. In truth, our human capacity for "reasonable dishonesty" has long been reached and exceeded.

Our fear of rejection seems to have outstripped our fear of deceit and its consequences. The hollowness of our faith in ourselves and the humanity of our fellow man has led us to avoid, evade, shade much of what passes our lips, all in the pursuit of acceptance. It is an empty victory at best, one that leads us to craft still more half-truths, make even more omissions, take the Fifth, so that we can cover the original sin and each of its off-spring. At the end of this twisted road, we are left facing ourselves, and we don't like the reflection that we see.

When we were children, Halloween gave us permission once a year to pretend to be someone entirely different. In our guises, we could become spookier, sillier, and rowdier, and our parents granted us more license than on most other days. As adults, some of us look forward to masked ball galas for the same reason; for one night, we want to live a different life under a different set of rules. At masquerade parties, part of the fun is trying to discern the identity of the character portrayed as well as that of the person behind the costume and makeup. After we're unmasked, we're sometimes astonished to see who was really there.

If you make the choice to live an authentic life based on who you really are rather than on who you think others want you to be, you will be unmasked on a daily basis, and you too will be astonished to see who was really there behind your mask all these years. I invite you to make this discovery.

For the last several years, there's been a boom in popular interest in spiritual matters, spawning a big business in lotions, potions, tapes, essential oils, tinctures, crystals, and other things that promise the consumer instant enlightenment. If you're true to yourself and others and you find serenity in using these products, that's all to the good. If you're not true to yourself or others and you use these products, the truth is that you are gift-wrapping garbage. The road to spiritual growth can take many paths: All are paved with the truth.

In my life, I discovered that truth is not like a "rolling stop" that you make at a stop sign. You really don't stop, in fact, but you know you should have. With regret, I have not always told the truth. In order to keep one person's confidence, I have had the discomfort of telling another person that I didn't have any information on a subject when, in fact, I did. I have arrived at a restaurant with no reservations and insisted that they existed and been seated with my party of six. And I have spread the occasional piece of spicy gossip. There is no advantage to this destructive behavior, but I have at least engaged in the dreaded self-examination, which leads to awareness and her sisters: accountability and action. Truth requires it. I know that dishonesty in one part of my life, however seemingly harmless, can eventually creep into all areas of my life. Deceit is a seductive siren.

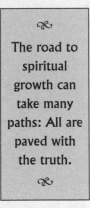

The road to spiritual growth can take many paths: All are paved with the truth.

Telling the truth is a spiritual pact: Why not invite God or another Divine Being to help you keep it? One of my friends knew that on a tough day, her character defect of manipulating the truth to her own ends was more likely to rear its ugly head than on others. She didn't like the consequences that deception seemed to engender—the resentments, distrust, broken relationships—plus her life experience had shown her that despite her slick maneuvers to make things go her way, she wasn't really in control of the ultimate outcome. So, on those days, before she got off the elevator and walked into her office, she'd look at the ceiling and say, "God, this is beyond me, it's in your hands." That acknowledgment seemed to help her to stay on the beam, to do her part and to resist the temptation to "finesse" the situation. (P.S. She also went through her day filled with more grace and serenity.)

Consider asking a close friend whose integrity you admire to hold you accountable. Ask her to call you on all forms of untruth: playing the victim rather than focusing on your part in the fiasco; telling a story that doesn't seem to add up; taking more than your fair share of the credit; making promises you can't possibly keep; leveraging your lifestyle with credit card debt; denying the reality of a situation; and skirting the real issue. It's a true-blue friend who will support this caliber of honesty, yet your request is also a gift to her for it allows her the opportunity to confront her fear of becoming the faithful mirror of truth for another. Real intimacy is grounded in nothing less.

Practice checkbook honesty. When you don't have enough money in the bank to write the check, let the payee know and make other arrangements. When the cashier at the grocery store gives you too much change, give it back. When the bartender offers to "buy back" your next drink, refuse the offer; unless he owns the bar, it's not his drink to give. When you don't have enough money to participate in a social activity, make plans to engage in one that is affordable. Truth asks you to check your ego at the door.

Living a life of integrity will require more than courage and support, it also demands patience. As Charles Hadon Spurgeon noted, "A lie travels around the world while Truth is putting on her boots." Living life on its terms and not bending them to meet your own means learning to take and accept things as they come. It usually does not offer instant gratification, but it's the only course that instills true gratification. Ultimately, a lie will cause you to trip, fall, and even fail.

For years, I have anxiously awaited "the rest of the story" from radio commentator Paul Harvey. I admire his poignant, analytical unfolding of the truth as he applies his wit and wisdom to each news segment of national and international note. As a messenger, he has my confidence that he'll make every attempt to unveil the truth—the whole truth. Wouldn't it be something if such honesty was nonnegotiable and we could restore public confidence in our mutual faith and trust?

> ❧
> "A lie travels around the world while Truth is putting on her boots."
> ❧

When living in Washington, D.C., I was chagrined by the major potholes that inevitably erupted after a severe winter season and threatened to throw my car out of alignment each spring. It was impossible to avoid every street with a large pothole looming and still reach my destination; there wasn't any way around it. In life, facing facts and telling the truth they reveal can look like a large pothole that threatens to rattle our smooth ride, and in our desire to pave an easier, softer way, we may use lies to cover them. It never works for long, if at all. Our hearts and souls are covered with each layer of deceit, and it closes them off from the sunlight of the Divine. We feel more burdened, our spirits fill with remorse and shame. Lies weave a heavy cloak.

You may have bright potential or be on your way up the ladder or have already arrived. You may look good, go to the right places, and have great references. But if you cannot tell the truth, you will lose all that you place before it. Make truth a priority in your life, let it shine through, and it will set you free!

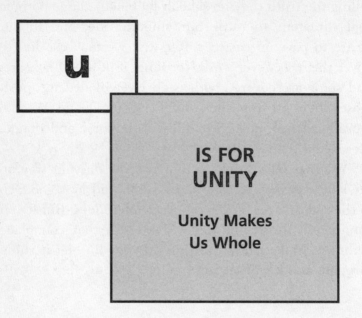

u

IS FOR
UNITY

Unity Makes
Us Whole

Through the generations, missions, movements,
causes, and crises have drawn people together to
work for their mutual preservation and advancement.
Both the towering and the tiny have responded in their
individual ways to make a shared statement of caring.
They have found that, quite often, human mathematics
is such that one plus one equals three, as one's strengths
join with another to forge a combination that's far
greater than the sum of its parts.

Before we can come together as a unified whole,
each of us first must understand, appreciate, and value

ourselves. As Stephen R. Covey, bestselling author and chairman of the Covey Leadership Center, says, "Interdependence is a higher value than independence, [but] effective interdependence can only be built on a foundation of true independence." This true independence is founded on a deep, abiding knowledge that you are enough. Does that ring true for you, or are you ill-at-ease, uncomfortable in your own skin? If so, ask yourself whether you are holding up someone else as the standard for what is acceptable rather than appreciating the gifts that you possess. Remember that one size does not fit all. Left-handed people write and think as well as right-handed people. People with brown eyes perform as well as people with blue eyes. People with blond hair can excel at the same rate as those with jet-black hair. The singer with the angelic soprano voice would be lost without the piano player. The gourmet big-city chef with the Midas touch would want for vital ingredients without the small-town farmer with the green thumb. Don't diminish your talents: Use them and you'll complement another person's gifts. The sum is always greater than the parts.

On a work team (or any team for that matter), it is a mistake to think that you are a Lone Ranger. You are never really alone. If you believe that you are, though, other people who could help you will respect your desire for independence and will leave you alone. Or they will resent your failure to acknowledge and honor their contributions and will freeze you out. Isolated, you will find yourself removed from wisdom, experience, and helpful hands that you otherwise could tap into. It is a weaker position.

If you've felt isolated or alone in your personal or professional life, here are some things you could try. The next time that "you" accomplish something at work, take time to consider all the people who played a part in the project and thank them for their contribution. If it's a project that unfolded over a long period of time, you might even get in touch with people who've moved on to other jobs and let them know about the successful completion. Everyone feels ownership for something that's involved him in some way, and, like you, other people crave recognition and receive far less of it than they'd like. Share the glory and it will be multiplied.

> ❧
> Share the glory and it will be multiplied.
> ❧

Strive to be big enough to do the small things. Understandably, you are important, busy, or preoccupied with all the things that are assigned to you, but take the time to jot a quick thank-you note. It is not a burden if you realize just how much it will mean to the recipient, and what it says about you as a person. People want to be acknowledged, remembered, and appreciated. A teacher of some thirty years was moved to tears as she read a letter from a student expressing his appreciation for all she had done to keep him in school and prevent him from becoming a negative statistic. He was the first student in her entire career who had ever written a word of thanks! Being in so many cities, I take pleasure in browsing through card shops and purchasing all types of note cards to send to people who deserve my standing ovation.

When you reflect on the achievement of any project, consider the so-called big players who led the initiative, the middle managers who kept things on track, and the workers whose extra mile possibly went unheralded. For example, during a long period of renovation in my office building, the construction crews worked from six in the evening until the early morning hours to keep from disrupting our workday. When the job was completed and the kudos were being handed out, right at the top of my personal list was the building maintenance man. For six months, he worked double duty, managing the building's operations during the normal working hours, keeping it open during the construction shift, and then getting it ready for a new work day. He did this all without complaint or fanfare and he won my appreciation and praise.

Taking time to notice and applaud the efforts of those who work behind the scenes and giving them credit for their contribution to the whole is personally very important to me. My own parents were domestic workers, and I recall the numerous times that they were complimented about their impeccable work for the upkeep of the buildings in which they worked. But there were also too many times when they were not viewed as an integral part of the team. We can't afford to let any contributors to a group effort feel like they're invisible or don't count, for soon they will be and they won't. Their ongoing active participation is needed for the good of the whole.

Many public school districts have won my heart with their decision to invite everyone who works for the district to attend the opening convocation ceremony. It is on this occasion that the district shares its vision for the coming year and leads the charge to inspire all to play their part. In some districts, only the administration and teaching staff are invited to the convocation. In those districts where the invitation is open to each and every school worker—from the bus driver who brings the children safely to school to the cafeteria worker who prepares their daily nourishment—there's a more global sense of shared unity and purpose that gives each institution within the district more strength and electricity.

> ✃
> Taking time to notice and applaud the efforts of those who work behind the scenes and giving them credit for their contribution to the whole . . .
> ✃

Accepting the value of teams in our heads is one thing; embracing it with our hearts is quite another. Who among us has never been assigned to work on a team with someone who truly rubs us the wrong way? Perhaps this person states his opinions loudly and repeatedly or practices character assassination on the side or doesn't pull his weight or all of the above. Regardless, it's not your job to make him vaporize (though you may wish it was); it is your job to work with him to accomplish the team's mission on time and on budget. To that end, each time you encounter this difficult person, try to lighten up and not take your personality differences so to heart. You might even try the rose-colored glasses game, where you look at him until you find one more thing about him that you like. As you focus steadily on his good qualities, you'll magically find that his less attractive traits will diminish in their importance to you.

If, despite your best efforts, this person becomes the veritable thorn in your side, regardless of who initiated the cold war, it's up to you to set things straight. Decide what you can do about it! That's right, you, and not Mr. Wrong. If you take the unilateral initiative to lay down your arms, you'll come out the winner on two levels: (1) the fight will be over (it takes two sides to fight, and you quit), and (2) you'll have the satisfaction of knowing that you were larger than a bad situation. He may not be able or willing to change, but your challenge is to find his best, match it with yours, and proceed.

Keep ever mindful of the wise maxim that warns, "The same people that you pass on the way up, you will pass on the way down." You need to work with, work for, get along with, and try to understand people. Most of all, you need to accept them as they are and resist giving them a makeover in your mind. Each of us has a unique role to play that is known only to God. Assuming that you have the authority to rewrite another's script is arrogant and wrong. Try to take each person as he or she comes and be grateful to those who extend the same generosity of spirit to you.

In the interest of unity, we all must surrender our need to have the last word. Ask yourself, "Would I rather be happy or right?" When you work with other people, success often hinges on holding that clever thought, biting your tongue, sitting on your hands, and deciding whether your contribution is really for the good of the team. Sometimes our ego-driven desire to strut our stuff can override our deeper interest in cooperation. Assess whether your impulse to debate resides on a self-righteous "It's the principle of the thing" and get real. Rather than speak up in that instance, sit back and cherish your silence as an opportunity to master your skills in working with and for all types of people.

Over the years, I have observed that those teams whose members had a strong passion for their shared mission, who sublimated their individual need to achieve, who were committed "just because" they were convinced the job needed to get done, were the most successful at meeting their goals. Often, but not always, these teams worked in the nonprofit arena and made incredible personal sacrifices to spend countless hours developing and executing programs that would uplift the less fortunate. Philosopher Immanuel Kant writes about the categorical imperative; it is a sense of "oughtness," he suggested, that makes us reach outside ourselves to help others. Shared mission feeds unity and gives it strength.

One friend of mine stumbled on the power of unity in a very unexpected way. She lost her job during the reengineering craze of the late 1980s when many people were out of work and openings were scarce. For a short period of time, she went to a support group for job seekers in New York City, and it kept her morale boosted. The gentleman who led the group was a former salesman for the *Wall Street Journal* who began the support group as a way of giving back to society. He encouraged everyone in the group to get out into the world and to enlist the support of all they encountered in their day. When asked, "How are you doing?" he encouraged them to answer "Great! I'm looking for a job in X with a company like Y," rather than the standard response of "Fine." It worked. Within one month of losing her job in the middle of a recession, by taking this unified approach to her job search, my friend landed a new job through an acquaintance who happened to know of a perfect opening. Six months into the new job, my friend returned to the old job seekers' forum to thank the participants there for their help and to encourage them that "if one door closes, a better one will open."

My friend learned in her job search an encouraging lesson about unity: You never know what someone has to offer you or the rest of the world. She took this powerful revelation with her into her new job and made a greater attempt to build relationships with each person there—regardless of the personality involved. She found that she enjoyed her work more than ever before and that she was far more productive. For the first time, she really felt as if she was part of a team that was working toward a common goal. And she knew that it wasn't a sudden shift in the world that was responsible for this change, it was a simple shift in her awareness.

For more than a decade, I have advocated "celebrating the differences" because it is the most pragmatic course of action. In business, community, and family, it is quite simply the competitive advantage. In some cultures, such as that of the Pueblo Indians, conscious attention is paid to the development of the community as a whole. Time is taken to make an inventory of the healthy growth of their unity. Think of your own community at work and beyond. Is it harmonious? Is there anything you can do to dissolve divisiveness? Remember that it is important that we seek to help, not hurt; to walk toward, rather than to walk away; to lift, not to limit; to pull together, rather than to pull apart; to listen, rather than to voice the last word. Unity begins with one. Unity begins with you.

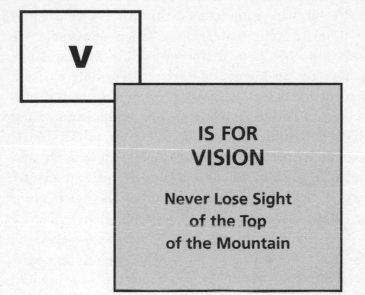

V

**IS FOR
VISION**

**Never Lose Sight
of the Top
of the Mountain**

Aim. Aim high. Aim high and follow your own vision straight to the top.

First, aim. Do you have a sense of where you want to go or do you draw a blank when you hear that question? If you can't picture where you'd like to be five years from now, do not stare harder; relax and turn your focus inward. Find a quiet place, close your eyes, and concentrate on visualizing the spot between your eyes. Notice what thoughts and images float through your mind. Try to imagine a place where you feel happy and fulfilled, then describe to yourself that place and how you see yourself therein. If you've been leading a very busy, task-oriented life with your focus on the short-term, it may take time for you to develop a vision statement. Be patient and have faith that it eventually will surface if you have the willingness to seek it. Forming a vision statement and deciding what you really care about means that you are the head writer of your autobiography, and each day is a brilliant new chapter.

Decide whom you want to become in your life and what legacy you'd like to leave behind. Do more than walk around with a vague vision in your mind or discuss it with a friend, family member, or team at work. A judge once approached me expressing his interest in joining the speaking circuit. He was a persuasive presenter, and he had convinced himself and me that he was serious about this career change. He talked to me for well over an hour about his ability and desire (I don't recall which one came first). My role, as he saw it, was to introduce him as a potential speaker to clients. I made one request of him: that he prepare a one-page background sheet that would support his attributes and suitability as a speaker. I am still waiting.

> ❧
> You are the head writer of your auto-biography, and each day is a brilliant new chapter.
> ❧

After careful thought and discussion, you need to reduce your inspiration for the future into a few crisp sentences, articulating your vision clearly so that your intent, purpose, plan, and preference are clear to you and all concerned. A vision statement might sound something like this:

- Build and manage an elegant nightclub where the nation's most talented cabaret entertainers will perform for appreciative, standing-room-only crowds.

- Help raise financing and provide business guidance for indigenous Caribbean basin entrepreneurs who supply good-quality products at fair prices for their local community's consumption.

- Become a pediatrician who provides high-caliber, preventive medical care to urban children via a storefront clinic in downtown Baltimore.

- Learn to read and speak French fluently and spend one year with my family living in Paris so that we can experience fully another culture and gain perspective on our roles in the global society.

Each of these vision statements differs greatly in most respects, but one thing they have in common is that they look well past the drafter's immediate circumstances; they describe what might be rather than what is. For example, the future Baltimore pediatrician is still working toward the completion of his dual MBA and MD degrees from Johns Hopkins University. In developing his vision statement, he allowed his imagination to move him forward—seeing far beyond the immediate moment— envisioning what can be; this young man's vision for tomorrow inspires his dedication to his studies today.

Commitment to a concrete vision statement is contagious. The young man who has the vision of owning an elegant supper club showcasing the top entertainers of the nation initially found that his friends thought that the idea was no more than sheer imagination. Over time, he showed that he was so consumed by his vision, so dedicated to his goal, and so articulate in its expression that, within a very short time, his friends had signed themselves up as "vision employees"!

Aim high. As you read your vision statement, you should feel yourself inspired and pulled upward where success awaits you, for a positive vision encourages you with the understanding that the way things are is not the way that they have to be. Many find it helpful to attach a higher purpose to their vision, so that its achievement will serve them as well as a greater community or divine good.

An effective vision statement raises the bar. When I'm working with groups of people, I immediately tell them to think "sky." I've found it allows them to free their minds of all the cobwebs of inhibitions and constraints, and to set aside what always has been for what can be. You can achieve more than your wildest dreams if you set your sights in that direction.

Remember the Harvard University experiment that uncovered the Pygmalion effect? The researchers studied fifty grade school teachers: Twenty-five were told their students were underachievers from apathetic families, and twenty-five were told their students were high achievers from supportive families. The scores of the purported underachievers dropped by 25–30 points, while the scores of the purported overachievers increased by 50 points. The only difference: the level of the teachers' expectations. The lesson: Expect more from yourself and you will reap more. Aim high, stay true, and take ownership of the possible.

Assume the best from yourself and others. When you demand a lot from yourself, those around you are likely to pick up their pace. Self-respect and hard work engender another's self-respect, your shared respect, and dedication. Looking for the best in others will help them to believe in themselves and their importance to accomplishing their part of your shared vision. Take time to applaud their strides with name recognition, professional acknowledgment, group presentation. Try to be as specific as possible in your compliments so that you are helping to reinforce their work in a constructive way (after all, your critique would probably be precise). Most of all, though, assume the best starting now!

There is no right or wrong vision statement. Each one is as individual as its creator. Think about life's possibilities as though they were colorful fragments in a beautiful kaleidoscope. As you look at them, you use your vision, your opinion of perfection, to adjust the kaleidoscope tube to the desired configuration. Likewise, your vision statement will bear your personal stamp, formed by your personality, preferences, creativity, and life experiences. It is your willingness and ability to take from your life experience that wisdom which, notwithstanding people or things that would seek to deter you, will lead you to a better tomorrow. Tom Peters, a leading management consultant, advises that a vision statement have "some give and take . . . so that you don't pull down the shades of opportunity and turn vision into blinders." Once you've crafted your statement, find a safe home for it where you can consult it on a regular basis and make adjustments as life introduces new challenges and opportunities. If not, you will be lost at sea, drifting aimlessly without the anchor of your thoughts and actions.

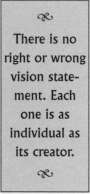

There is no right or wrong vision statement. Each one is as individual as its creator.

I am often asked, "How long did it take you to write the speech?" My honest response: "All of my life!" Each speaking effort requires that I pull on all of my life experiences to shape my remarks to meet the target audience. It is then that I can share with them what I have learned, why, and how, as well as which strategies worked and which ones failed. Your vision statement will be formed and re-formed in much the same way.

Follow your vision. Consider a road trip that leads five hundred miles to your destination. Before you get on the road, you probably will look at road maps to guide your selection of the route. You might even break the trip down into segments, with planned rest stops along the way. You'll probably build extra time into your scheduled arrival so that you have the luxury of taking any extra breaks if the journey becomes too arduous. At each stop, planned and otherwise, you can check your progress against your envisioned destination, see how it's going, and adjust your vision accordingly. Such is the way that you can implement your vision statement.

If your vision involves assuming the helm of your department within the next five years, for example, and you're currently sitting in a cubicle, you need to plot out all the steps between the two and start taking them today. For instance, you'll need to get a sense of the skills the corner office will require, figure out how to acquire those skills, and start amassing them. You'll also need to build positive working relationships, demonstrate a commitment to the CEO's corporate vision, work smart, and maintain a record that can withstand scrutiny. It would also be savvy to get involved with the local, state, or national professional organization within your industry and to find a mentor whose success you wish to emulate. And, frankly, you'll also have to do some careful politicking to make sure that your value is apparent to those who can boost your progress up the ladder. You need to start now; remember, "Life is not a dress rehearsal."

Do you plan out your day in the morning or the evening before? It's a good discipline to get into. As you map out your plan for the day, you might consider keeping your vision statement close at hand. After you've drafted out the day's events, see how they measure up against your vision for the future. Find out if you can include at least one step, task, or project that will inch you closer to the achievement of your vision. You might even consider preplanning and scheduling some project steps across the days and weeks that lie ahead. Use the organizational skills that serve you so well in the office and household to help you achieve your personal dreams.

The Bible is instructive: "Where there is no vision, the people perish." Open your eyes and put these rules in play today. Craft your vision in your head. Work on your vision from your heart.

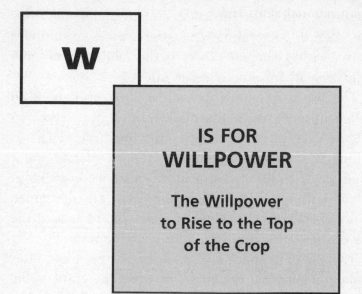

W

IS FOR
WILLPOWER

**The Willpower
to Rise to the Top
of the Crop**

Exercising your willpower is all about maximizing your true potential. It's about giving all your undertakings your best shot because everything you do represents you. It's about dodging the daily worry, fear, instigators, and invaders (internal or external) that threaten to detour you off the path to your destination. Most of all, it's about shifting out of park and switching on your personal power. It's about paying the price at the tollbooth, because the endless stretch of highway on the other side is well worth the trip!

Willpower! The word is so potent that it is worthy of

exegesis. According to Webster's New Dictionary and Thesaurus, will is the "attitude, choice, command, decision, desire, determination, prerogative, resolution, resolve, wish"; whereas power is the "ability to do anything; capacity for producing an effect."

The two words together, willpower, then denote an applied attitude, productive choice, the ability to do anything at your command. Incredible, but true. There is nothing mysterious, magical, remote, or exclusive about willpower. It is simply the capacity that we each have, every day, to make the most of our innate and developed talents in achieving our desires. It is a loud knock at the door of your being that shouts, "One more round!"

The human experience consists of one event after another and another and just one more; therefore, being energized and willing to face the next project, initiative, or difficulty is essential. You can be assured that the next test or opportunity is just a few steps behind. Stand ready with a surfeit of willpower and an unwavering commitment to make a solid effort. Remember the words of Robert Frost, "The best way out is always through."

In college, there were more than a few days when I thought that the easiest, if not best route for me, was to go into a holding pattern. At the time, I did not consider quitting school, but I would toy with the idea of lightening my load, generally using the rationalization that fewer courses would enable me to better balance and execute all my responsibilities. In actuality, I could successfully handle the load I was carrying but I was momentarily fatigued, and, subliminally, the take-it-easier way began to try to seduce my subconscious mind. Luckily, I would catch myself and use positive self-talk to rally my spirits. I would tell myself, "You can do it" or "It takes willpower to do what you need to do" or "You've got to be in it to win it." Then I'd buckle back down with my studies and the self-doubt would pass.

We all have the responsibility to pay attention to the messages we send ourselves. Sometimes, without being conscious of it, we sabotage our efforts through negative self-talk. If you're feeling paralyzed, maybe you are being held hostage by the self-talk that says, "If ever I have the chance to . . ." which becomes dwarfed by a long list of "if onlys." Or maybe you are stuck in a rut, frozen by convincing self-talk that says that you dare not take a chance or you might make a mistake. The person who has never made a mistake is a person who has never achieved very much. There is no glory in not trying. Don't let your self-talk worry you into not taking the next step.

> ❧
> The person who has never made a mistake is a person who has never achieved very much.
> ❧

Let's stop for a moment and look at worry because this distress signal is the one that most often impedes your progress. Experts who have studied worry have found that more than 90 percent of our worries never materialize. Looked at another way, this means that our worst fears have only a 10 percent chance of happening.

Sometimes the worries that are festering in our minds concern things that are completely out of our control.

You must admit, if you spend a lot of time worrying about something over which you are utterly powerless, it is not a good use of your time. It would be far better to spend your energies coming up with creative solutions to those things you can influence. So it is important to keep the range of your willpower in perspective. Here's an exercise that will help develop that awareness. Make a list of ten things that fall within your willpower and ten things that don't:

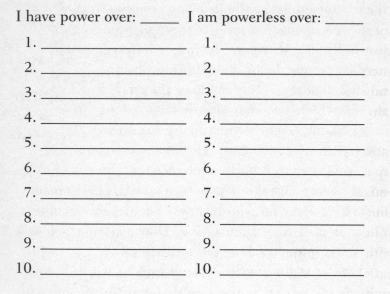

I have power over: _____   I am powerless over: _____

1. _____   1. _____

2. _____   2. _____

3. _____   3. _____

4. _____   4. _____

5. _____   5. _____

6. _____   6. _____

7. _____   7. _____

8. _____   8. _____

9. _____   9. _____

10. _____   10. _____

Did you have a hard time coming up with ten different things that fall completely under your control? Were you surprised? The first time I did this exercise, it was such an eye-opener because I suddenly realized that all I really control pretty much boils down to what goes into my mind and comes out of my mouth. And it made me appreciate those areas of my life where I have some power even if it's not complete, and it gave me new incentive to exert my will in making positive choices in those areas when possible. For example, though I can't will other people to do things my way, in my free time, I can choose with whom I associate and I can gravitate toward those individuals who contribute positively to my emotional, physical, intellectual, and spiritual development. And though I can't dictate how every dollar I earn is spent (just ask Uncle Sam), I can make conscious choices about my spending and saving habits. The point is to develop your awareness of where exerting your will will make a difference and where its dogged application will only frustrate you and all involved. Though you are powerless over certain things in your life, you are never helpless.

Sometimes, when I feel my willpower wavering, rather than using positive self-talk, I close my eyes and try a little creative visualization. The same can work for you. If you're running a race and beginning to slow down, think of yourself standing on the victor's stand and watch yourself catch a second wind. Or if you're struggling with your studies for that degree or professional certification, imagine yourself wearing your mortarboard on graduation day or framing your new certificate for your office wall. Or if you're sweating the next job interview, imagine yourself celebrating the successful completion of your first project at the new company with your teammates.

Acceptance and affirmation are two additional ways of shoring up your willpower. In terms of acceptance, I have learned that things are as they are for a reason, and that I gain information and fortitude from going through what I never imagined I would successfully be able to manage. I also believe, and this is true for you too, that if the problems or circumstances were less difficult, there would be no need to have someone with my ability to solve them. Another way people sometimes express this is "God never gives you more than you can handle."

> ☙
>
> **If the problems or circumstances were less difficult, there would be no need to have someone with my ability to solve them.**
>
> ☙

(Though in my cloudy moments, I sometimes prefer the rejoinder "God sure does have a good sense of humor!")

Accepting that I am up to facing the challenge serves as a powerful affirmation and gives me a surge of fresh determination. If you're feeling very overwhelmed and need to switch your willpower back on, try this: Take a seat at your mental computer. Press the restore key to reinstate any self-talk that keeps you encouraged, convinced, and determined. Change the font size to bold, 36-point type and write "YES, I CAN!"

Another technique worth trying: Create a collection of flash cards containing positive affirmations. If you're going through a stressful time in your life, you might think about starting out your day in the company of these cards. Inscribe them with sayings like "I am a beautiful person inside and out," "I am open to receive all the gifts life brings today," "I am a powerful person with a meaningful message to convey," and "I love all whom I encounter and they return my love without condition." One friend of mine has a stack of one hundred affirmation cards that she's created over time. Every morning, she randomly pulls ten cards from the stack, reads each one out loud three times, and silently ponders its meaning. If upon completing her reading, she feels any negativity, she makes her way back through the stack. She continues in that fashion until all the negative self-talk has quieted and her will is renewed.

Don't allow yourself to be susceptible to the negativity of others. When someone says you can't, you can—until you think you can't. When facing contention, train your energies on identifying the like-minded and strengthening the consensus. When you feel overwhelmed—and everyone does at some point—renew, take sanctuary, but don't retire. I was once the facilitator for an intense leadership training weekend for college coeds. The question was asked, "What do you do when you are worn out from being a leader?" My answer was, "Rest. Renew. Return to the front lines!"

> ❧
> When someone says you can't, you can—until you think you can't.
> ❧

Remember the last time you thought you had nothing left to give, but you dug deeper and you gave still more. There is always a deeper dimension to what you can do. Draw strength from this wise Chinese proverb: "Great souls have wills; feeble ones have only wishes." Create a "victory file," a collection of souvenirs from experiences when you overcame despite all odds. Make a list. On the left-hand side, list all the times when you contemplated giving up, quitting in discouragement, yielding to the competition, or taking half measures. In the middle column, note what action you took and the result. Then in the right-hand column, state why the situations in your first column became a benchmark, an obstacle, or an opportunity. Build from your past success and remember that it will return as long as you don't turn around midstream, throw in the towel, and decide that failure is imminent, that all hope is lost, or that the obstacles are too great.

> ❧
> Remember the last time you thought you had nothing left to give, but you dug deeper and you gave still more.
> ❧

Get into the habit of saying this positive, personal, present tense, emotional affirmation: "This is nothing!" And, whatever it is, it actually becomes nothing when you are so self-motivated in the way you address it. It's an incredible booster shot for your will. Just look at the list of situations and people that you can handle, if you are willing to believe, and then act on your belief that "This is nothing!"

Situation 1: You get bypassed for your dream job.
Response: "This is nothing! Thank goodness there is a job market—not just one job!"

Situation 2: You did not get called for a second interview.
Response: "This is nothing! There's a better job waiting for me. This one helped me to hone my interviewing skills so I'll be ready when the right opportunity arises."

Situation 3: The blind date turns out to be a jerk within the first five minutes of your meeting.

Response: "This is nothing! At least I have friends who are willing to set me up on dates. There are more fish in the sea. I'll get out more and check out my options."

Situation 4: You don't pass your professional certification exam.

Response: "This is nothing! The tests are administered year round. I'll take a review course and ace it the next time around."

Situation 5: You feel stuck in a life filled with ceaseless gray.

Response: "This is nothing! All I need to do is change channels; the remote's in my hand."

Situation 6: Unhealthy, unhappy (dysfunctional) people seek to invalidate you.

Response: "This is nothing! Everybody has limitations, especially those who attack another person. I wish for them all the blessings I would have for myself."

Situation 7: You were asked to train the person who was hired to be your new supervisor.

Response: "This is nothing! This gives me an opportunity to show myself and others my value to the company. Maybe I'll even discover that I myself am capable of a supervisory role, and then I can take steps toward a promotion.

Situation 8: You lost your job.
Response: "This is nothing! I'll have a few days off between engagements and an opportunity to locate a different and even better opportunity.

Situation 9: You find yourself blaming others for your woes.
Response: "This is nothing! Other people don't have it out for me. I need to look inward and discover why my spiritual condition and faith are so shaken."

Situation 10: You find yourself lost on a city street.
Response: "This is nothing! I have a great sense of direction that will lead me back home to safety."

A friend of mine has her own variation of "This is nothing!" When she finds herself getting vexed, when she finds herself having arguments with people who aren't in the same room, when frustration threatens to cut off her forward motion, she says two simple words: "So what!" Like my "This is nothing!" it helps her to get things back into proper perspective and strengthens her resolve.

You know, it's easy to persevere (or easier) when we've made a popular choice and we find ourselves surrounded by cheerleaders. The real test of our willpower comes, however, when we trudge doggedly forward alone and even against the tide. In my case, my early efforts to perfect my declarative speech and oratorical style were not always understood, much less supported. I lived through many childhood days when others were playing games or at parties and I was on the porch rehearsing my speech. I didn't let it deter me. My toys became my listening audience. Now my three- to four-doll audience has been replaced by thousands of people in banquet halls and convention centers across the land. Like me, fasten your talent and dreams to your willpower and the possible, then watch it all come true.

On those days, when things aren't going your way, when you feel as if your words have fallen on deaf ears, your plans have failed, your friends do not understand, your efforts are discarded, your contributions are under a cloud, your savings have evaporated, and your bad choices seem to tip the scales in the wrong direction, don't give up. Reach down to your deep, rich reserve of willpower and pull it up. Then lift up your hand and head. Share your trial with the One in whom you believe. Don't expect a sign or a psychic prediction in response, giving you a trend or projection. After all, your communication is not a toll call. But you can expect the answer to come, and it will probably be transmitted through the mouth of another person. It will reassure you that you have the will to do anything within your power that you want to do.

You must have the courage of your own convictions and the tenacity to remain undeterred. I was speaking in Soweta, South Africa, and I made a decision to use only three words in my address. Simply, "Never, Never, Never, Never, Never, Never, Never, Never, Never, Never Give Up!" "Never Give Up!" They haven't, nor will I, nor shall you.

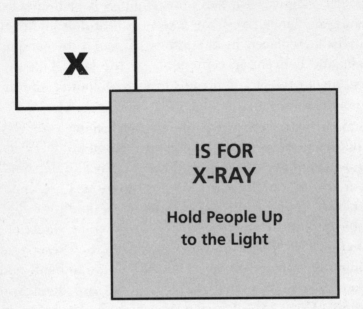

X

**IS FOR
X-RAY**

**Hold People Up
to the Light**

Take nothing at face value. That was one of the most valuable lessons of my legal training. We were taught to question and examine everything, to leave no stone unturned, for you never know where the most valuable piece of evidence might lie. That training has aided me not only in my professional career but also in my personal relationships. It has encouraged me to always look beyond the first impression, for that's where the truth of someone's humanity and worth really lies.

Pretend that you have X-ray vision and use it to peel back the masks and layers and walls so that you can see

all the good residing in others. Hold all their best qualities up to the light so that they sparkle and grow. This is
not to say that you remain blind to any of their character
defects. Rather, you want to strive to go through life with
the open eyes of one who sees everything,
overlooks most, and criticizes little. This
humble path is an easy one to take when
you remain mindful of the fact that we each
have our own imperfections. Or as one of
my friends put it more bluntly, "I try to
remember that I'm just another bozo on the
bus."

> ❧
> I once said to
> a friend, "I'm
> so selfish."
> To which
> he wisely
> responded,
> "Pat, you are
> many things."
> ❧

Each of us carries a mixed bag into the
game of life. We have some personality
traits that are helpful, others that are hurt-
ful; we have habits that are courteous, others that are
disagreeable; we have attitudes that are open and flexible, others that are closed and cantankerous; we are
know-it-all at times, know-nothing at others; we have
insight and blind spots; we bring encouragement and
discouragement; and we are friendly at times, chilly at
others. In a flash of self-disgust, I once said to a friend,
"I'm so selfish." To which he wisely responded, "Pat, you
are many things."

We are many things: We are not one-dimensional or
single-faceted. So, think about it, when you see someone
and you size him up quickly, you are using one freeze-
frame of one brief moment in one day of his whole life to
pass judgment on his entirety. Who loses? Is it the one
judged as this or that because he was behaving this or

that way for one instant? Or is it the judge who arrogantly labels another human being with one small tag when it would take many volumes to make an accurate description? Next time, look again, and again, and again, and the outlines of a new friend may begin to take form before your very eyes. Reserve judgment: Preserve a friendship.

Observe. When you first meet other people, strive to look into their eyes and truly acknowledge them. Study their dress to see if there's a point of pride that provides a clue to their interests. Maybe she's wearing a dog pin of the breed she fancies. Or perhaps he's wearing an antique watch that belonged to his grandfather, who is one of his biggest heroes. Or maybe she's wearing a hand-knit scarf that's one of the first she ever made. Or he's wearing a really sharp hat from his vast collection. Take time to notice and to acknowledge these details. Ask gentle, open-ended questions about your observations and draw out their personality. Refuse to engage again in commonplace pleasantries where no real information about the person before you is exchanged. Life is too short to miss out on an opportunity to really connect with a new person!

Reserve judgment: Preserve a friendship.

Observe their surroundings. When you first enter someone's office or home, you will find yourself surrounded with clues about his deepest passions and concerns. Take the clues and ask for more. Do you notice lots of souvenirs lining the shelves? Then you are in the presence of an adventurous spirit with colorful stories to divulge. Ask about the stories behind some of her prized trophies. Are there a few carefully framed photographs of family members hung neatly on the wall? You might be face-to-face with someone who places family ties first and foremost in his life. Ask after the welfare of his children and loved ones, and watch him come to life! Or maybe you see the walls of a study lined from pillar to post with well-thumbed books on a range of subjects. Take a look for topics that are of common interest and you've found your common spark. A person's possessions do have tales to tell about his past and present; often, though, it's up to you to take the lead and draw him out. Taking a sincere interest in another person's interests is a tremendous gift to bestow. Start giving it.

Observe their potential. In our relationships with others, we truly do have a divine obligation to bring out the best, not the worst, in others. If in your interactions, therefore, your critical mind is trying to laser in on all the wrong/bad things about other people, you risk concentrating on and accentuating those negative qualities. Instead, use your enormous creative powers to look between the lines, to listen to what could be, to hear their dreams and aspirations and to imagine a bridge that will carry them there. Remember too that they grow and change: The person before you today will not be the same person you face tomorrow. Think about antiques shopping when you are unable to evaluate the intrinsic value—the years may have taken a toll, but the true value has actually greatly increased. People experience victories and valleys and both give them a new worth, and attach a deeper meaning to their lives.

A couple of years ago, a popular book called *The Rules* was a runaway bestseller with its promise to share with women the exact way that they had to go about landing a husband. Well, I'm not going to make that promise here. What I will do is take you through some sticky situations that you might encounter in your relationships—professional, platonic, or romantic—and then we'll look at them with our X-ray eyes.

> **Sticky situation 1:** You hear through the grapevine that a coworker is jealous of you and is stabbing you in the back.
>
> **X-ray look:** MRI is a diagnostic procedure of modern medicine that doctors use to detect injury or illness. While it doesn't work on the human personality, jealousy, gossip, consistent insults, and deceit are all sure signs that a person is among the walking wounded. In your encounters with this person, think of her as you would a critically sick person. Treat her with kindness, look for the good in her, and wish her well. Take care to always act, not react, in her presence. Take the high road.
>
> **Sticky situation 2:** One of your best friends has begun to e-mail and call you every day at the office. She seems to need and want a lot more attention than you are comfortable giving.

X-ray look: At different stages in every relationship, each participant's needs shift. Perhaps this friend is encountering some uncertainty in her professional or romantic life, and so she's eager to cling more tightly to those people she knows she can count on. Rather than terminating the friendship, talk to her and let her know that you've noticed that she's been reaching out more often. Ask her why. Let her know that she can count on you for support but set honest parameters that will be comfortable for you to respect.

Sticky situation 3: A boss refuses to look up from his work when you go into his office to meet with him, and he often walks off in the middle of your sentence. **X-ray look:** Accept that, for now, this person is in charge and it's up to you to dance to his tune. See if you can manage your conduct around his behavior. For example, maybe you've been dropping by his office for impromptu meetings and he prefers a scheduled appointment. Or perhaps you need to get to the point more quickly and keep your communications brief to show respect for his time. At the next appropriate time, a six-month evaluation or a private meeting, ask him what you can do to facilitate a great working relationship. Also look for clues in his positive interactions with others: Are they doing anything different from you?

Sticky situation 4: An employee doesn't listen to your oral instructions.

X-ray look: For many years I worked with an employee who was an anxious listener, always finishing my sentences for me, shaping them into what she thought I would have said and missing any correction thereof. She had a lot going for her, and I sensed that part of her anxious listening style came from her eagerness to get everything done just right. While I was convinced that I couldn't change her verbal communication style, I did find a way to work with it. Whenever I needed to set forth instructions for a project, I did so in writing. That way, both sides knew exactly what was transmitted and nothing was lost in the proverbial translation. It worked.

Sticky situation 5: You join a new organization and begin immediately to share all your helpful new ideas: Your enthusiasm meets resistance from every corner. **X-ray look:** A key fact about human personality: As much as people say they're open to change and welcome a new face, it truly frightens them, even if they're not absolutely crazy about the way things were. If you want to build a consensus around your new initiatives, take it slow and make sure you have buy-in from all the influential players. Try to get a feel for the organization's history, so they'll know your suggestions are based in knowledge and aren't random. You'll find that on some points, you'll have to go along to get along. Realize too that there is an advantage to embracing the thoughts and ideas of those persons who are not on your side. It is better to keep them very close to you, rather than to have them plotting a strategy against you from a distance.

Sticky situation 6: You share some private information with someone in confidence, only to find that variations on the theme have been broadcast all over town.
X-ray look: Assume that your friend or associate convinced herself that it would do no harm to share this piece of information with others. Hold your tongue until any residual anger or hurt has passed. Then ask this person for a cup of coffee or tea. Seek to understand why the breach occurred and to let her know your feelings about the matter without attacking or passing judgment on her behavior. Forgive her just as others have forgiven you in your moments of poor judgment.

Sticky situation 7: You are surprised when someone takes offense at what you intended as an innocuous comment.
X-ray look: All of us hear things in our own fashion. We filter the words spoken through our past experience and education, through our observation of the body language and vocal tone, through any judgments we attach to the speaker's race, color, creed, or gender. By the time the message reaches our ears, it's been transformed. The key here is not to try to invalidate the other person's reaction. He heard what he heard. Acknowledge his hurt feelings, apologize for your part in it, and move on. If you consistently find that you're sending mixed messages to many people, you might want to check and see whether your body language or

your voice—tone, volume, speed—is contributing to the confusion.

Sticky situation 8: A group of volunteers seems dispirited and lacks motivation to get behind the organization's cause.

X-ray look: People respond well to structure and discipline. Often, in charitable environments where the workers are volunteering their time, the leadership feels they can't impose many rules or demands, and so the volunteers drift along and eventually abandon ship. Let me share an impressive strategy that was employed so that all board members of a nonprofit would take ownership of their roles and responsibilities and put forth the expected level of commitment. Board members were asked to take thirty minutes and actually review the specific obligations of their appointment. Then they were asked to write a four- to five-point contract of intent. Finally, they were to date and sign the agreement. They were, of course, responsible for enforcing it themselves. Even so, it ignited the board with a new level of dedication and purpose that we'd never seen before.

Sticky situation 9: You have delegated important tasks, they are not completed, and you are left holding the bag (or briefcase).

X-ray look: People have good intentions but life sometimes throws a curve ball disrupting the completion of the task. In the law, this is called a "superseding, intervening cause." Acknowledge to yourself and all involved that it's important to have a Plan B in place and to communicate if or when Plan A looks like it's going by the boards so that you can all switch tack. Let me share an example. My team had a very important meeting with a corporate executive, and we were assembling at his headquarters from our field offices around the country. It was winter, so we devised a plan that would accommodate late arrivals and no arrivals. We agreed that each team member, even in the absence of the team leader, would be totally prepared to give the entire presentation on his or her own! Although everyone arrived on time, we were prepared, just in case.

You may have experienced or been poised to experience some or all of the sticky situations just described. If so, you've probably found you can manage them most effectively if you train your focus on the actual circumstance that requires your concentration and resist making value judgments about the other person's behavior or motive.

Here's something that's helped me to put many sticky situations with people into their proper perspective. Imagine that you are taking a Concorde jet into the future. Your point of destination is an unencumbered place. There are no "problem people," there are no assignments and projects to review or revise, and there are no deals to negotiate or things to get through. This current situation will have become a dim or nonexistent memory. You have to ask yourself, in ten years from now or even next week, "What difference does this really make?" Respond accordingly.

I do not recommend using an X-ray on another person's mind. If you think you know what he's thinking about you or anyone or anything else, for that matter, you're probably dead wrong. That's where assumptions can become so treacherous and misleading. Take the time to invite the other person to tell you directly what he is thinking about a subject. He'll appreciate the opportunity to state his views, and you'll be operating with a full deck rather than a wild card.

Enter the laboratory of your daily life, take your microscope, and read the film. Record your findings—who and what you see. Then, determine what the goals and timetables are; anticipate which people will cross your path on this day (e.g., coworkers, family, or friends); and decide how you will work with each person to coexist, with understanding and harmony.

Remember, in seeking to master the "people game," rarely can you win, but it is essential to try. There are many variables. Hold people up to the light and decide that you will talk it through, that you can make a fair assessment of your relationship, and that you can always arrive at an amicable solution. Playing hide and seek does not produce answers.

Hold people up to the light—both as they are and how they can become. See everything, overlook most, criticize little.

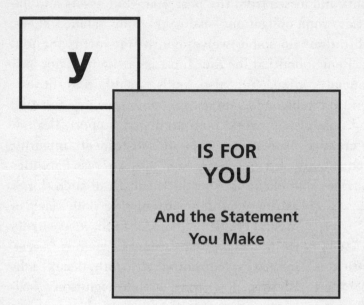

y

IS FOR
YOU

And the Statement
You Make

Many people entered into the stock market for the first time in the past decade. Most looked to buy into mutual funds that were beating the market or index funds that seemed to promise safer returns. Some even ventured into stock picking. All have had their ups and downs. Here's a hot tip for all you investors: I have a hunch that many of you have missed out on making the hottest investment of all: you.

Think about yourself as if you were a small, closely-held company called You, Inc. Now go to your book-keeper and ask her to make an accounting of all your

profits and losses from the past year, your assets and liabilities, your obligations sitting on your balance sheet,
and to draw up some twelve-month statements for You,
Inc. Remember that for You, Inc., assets include not only
financial capital, but also skills, health and fitness,
friends, intelligence, ability to communicate, spiritual
condition, charity work, community of support, flexibility, creative expression, level of self-respect, integrity,
responsibility, and emotional quotient; whereas liabilities
(ooh, we don't like to look at this!) consist of such things
as financial debt, atrophying skills, lack of
mental challenge, lack of faith, insensitivity
to others, possessiveness, jealous anger,
inability to communicate, sloth, deceit, self-
ishness, downward mobility, gluttony, laziness, and greed. Take a careful look at the
statement that You, Inc., makes. Is it the
sort of statement that you'd like to make?

> ❧
> Think about
> yourself as
> if you were
> a small,
> closely held
> company
> called
> You, Inc.
> ❧

The bull market for You, Inc., begins
with you. Think about all the news reports
you've read about the incredible bull market that we've experienced. Most financial
experts attribute the trend to corporate excellence and
investor faith (they're called "bullish") in their continuing potential for growth and success. The bull market
represents millions of individuals doing their part to
manage well, create high-quality products and services,
set the trends, respond to consumers, and remain agile
in the marketplace. Conversely, the bear market reflects
the opposite: As a consequence of a series of missteps

and failures, the market value is retreating. Perhaps management is using an outmoded strategy, the quality of goods and services has eroded, fresh capital investment has shrunk, products are obsolete, customers are ignored. Worst of all, investors' confidence has slumped; they've become "bearish." The upward or downward trend reflects the culmination of choices and actions for You, Inc.; all those choices and actions are firmly in your control.

When it comes to You, Inc., are you "bullish" or "bearish" about the future? In making this decision, it is important to look at your stock alone. Don't compare yourself to others and don't wonder how others view your prospects. They are not the key determinants of your future; you are. Instead, look squarely at what investments you have made and are planning to make in You, Inc. Except where indicated, evaluate the amount of money or time dedicated to the particular asset on a monthly basis, as you complete the following inventory:

Asset	Activity Amount or Time Dedicated
Savings per annum	_____
Debt repayment per annum	_____
Current investment portfolio (total principal invested)	_____
New investment per annum	_____
Mortgage per annum	_____

Asset   **Activity Amount**
                                          or Time Dedicated *(cont)*

Communication skills   _____
  (note your oral and written proficiency
  and computer literacy and what
  you're doing to enhance these assets)

Professional skills   _____
  (note those talents that ensure your
  success and indicate what you're
  doing to enhance these assets)

Health/nutritionq   _____
  (note preventive care, sleep, addictions,
  stress management, as well as diet)

Fitness/exercise   _____
  (note strength building, flexibility,
  cross training, and endurance work)

Intellectual capital   _____
  (note your intake of intellectually
  stimulating classes and books)

Spiritual condition   _____
  (note commitment to regular spiritual practices
  such as meditation, prayer, inspirational
  reading and work with a spiritual mentor)

Developing friendships and   _____
  community (note time and activities
  devoted to enriching old relationships
  and building new ones; pay attention
  to the amount or lack of diversity that
  exists herein and look for ways to grow)

Family life   _____
   (note time and activities dedicated to
   developing immediate and extended
   family ties)

Charitable works   _____
   (note all the ways you tithe your time,
   money, and resources, and think about
   additional ways you can benefit society)

Personal flexibility/adaptability   _____
   (note how often you try new things
   —whether it's a different restaurant,
   a new way of wearing an old shirt, a
   different seat at the dinner table,
   exploring a new town—and look
   for growth activities in this area)

Creative expression   _____
   (note books, classes, and time
   involved in honing your personal
   creative expression or in admiring/
   encouraging that of others)

Emotional intimacy   _____
   (note commitment you make to
   developing a deeper, more honest
   communication with the most
   significant people in your life; list
   books, classes, support groups, and
   other activities that are helping to
   develop this asset)

You can, if you like, also draw up an inventory of your liabilities. It will give you quick insight into some traits that might be getting in your way. A word of caution, though: Don't fall into the trap of so many who obsess so fiercely over a minor character flaw (such as lack of punctuality) that they forget to build on their strengths. As you become aware of a character defect that no longer serves you (such as indecisiveness), make a steadfast commitment to making a decision, and ask your friends and God to help you uphold that commitment. Do not make working on eradicating your defects, however, the sine qua non of your existence. In terms of personal development, you will make your greatest gains if you work from your strength and use the inventory of your assets to first guide you toward any changes needed in the management of You, Inc.

Once a year, most companies invest several weeks in the creation of a strategic plan and budget. It sets forth an accounting of how the current year is stacking up, predicts forthcoming market conditions, assesses strategic assets and liabilities, and then draws up a target of goals and initiatives to achieve for the coming year. When the companies undertake this planning depends on whether they're on a fiscal or calendar year and whether they like to lay out their plans well in advance of the new business year's onset or have a just-in-time mindset. I'm going to recommend that You, Inc., draw up its strategic plans right now.

If you're like a lot of people, the extent of your annual strategic planning consisted of making a few

New Year's resolutions. Perhaps you resolved to get a better job or to lose weight or to find the man or woman of your dreams or to take an exciting vacation. In any case, unless you created a real plan to realize those dreams (e.g., set up a vacation savings account and designated a portion of each paycheck for that account, or joined a health club and made an iron-clad commitment to work out thrice weekly), then they'll remain just that, dreams. How many years did I make the resolution with groups of friends to eat better, lose weight, and get in shape? Unless I put real steps, action, and discipline behind those words, they remained an empty promise. Plus, even if I did work on my health and fitness asset, unless I took steps to develop my other assets, my investment in myself would be lopsided.

As the chairman and CEO of You, Inc., you must draw up a comprehensive strategic plan for the next twelve months that includes strategies and goals for taking each of your assets to the next level. If you've taken an inventory of your assets, you've made an important step toward creating this plan. In working through that inventory, you probably uncovered a lot of clues about where you need to invest more time and resources; that's actually very exciting information. Now that you have the awareness, you can take the actions that will drive You, Inc.'s stock to an all-time high. For example, maybe your inventory uncovered a shortfall in the development of your intellectual capital. In your plan, you can think of rewarding and fun ways that you can introduce more mental challenge into your life and then add those activities to your plan. As you come up with these goals, it's important that you develop realistic ones that challenge but don't overwhelm you. If you've been feeding your mind a steady diet of television, shopping catalogs, weekly news, and the occasional bestseller, for instance, it might be unrealistic to commit yourself to reading a work of literary merit once a week and enrolling in a continuing education course in Russian. Think about small strides that stretch rather than break you, such as joining a friendly book club so that you're motivated to read a book a month (plus you're developing your community support asset at the same time!) and swapping one hour of weekly sitcom watching for one hour of educational television. Remember, each moment that you invest in your mind is never lost. As that wise saying put it, "Once a mind is stretched, it never returns to the original position."

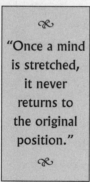

"Once a mind is stretched, it never returns to the original position."

Once you've drafted your strategic plan and made sure that achievable and respectable goals are set for each asset, ask yourself, "Am I excited about carrying out this plan?" Your enthusiasm for your prospects will go a long way toward fueling your success. Also, you need to make sure that your strategic plan reflects your core vision and values; if it hews closely, you're assured of meeting its demands. And I predict that You, Inc., will have a banner year!

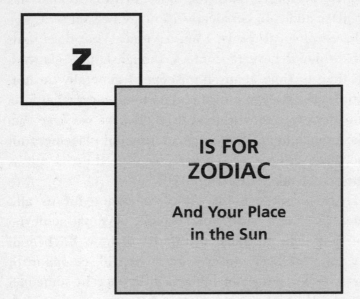

Z

IS FOR ZODIAC

And Your Place in the Sun

On the night or day of your birth, all the stars and planets aligned just so, and you became a cosmic reality. You took your place in the galaxy. Overhead, in the Milky Way alone, more than 225 billion stars probably shone brightly. And, according to some scientific estimates, as many as 50 million different extraterrestrial civilizations were already thriving in the same galaxy. You became a small yet significant part of an incredible universe.

Your daily footsteps can be sure, not dubious. After all, you are not earthly bound. You are a child of the universe. If you forget that, just look up; you'll remember your place and gain perspective. You are heaven sent.

In astrological terms, I am a Virgo. What does that mean to me? I have to confess, though I have glanced from time to time at my horoscope, I generally do not scrutinize the daily readings and try to discover what fate lies in store for me. In life, I firmly believe we have the stellar probability of finding our terrestrial placement in those places where we propel ourselves. Life is not a magic carpet ride, but I will take it.

There is not one big cosmic meaning for us all. Rather, there is a variety of purpose, personal achievement, and calls to make a difference, now. Each and every day, if we keep our eyes open, we will see opportunities, small or large, to make a difference in someone else's life. When I sign my name, I often write the word *Strength*. For well or ill, up or down, employed or unemployed, I know that people have struggles and I want them to know that I wish them strength on their journey. A friend of mine always signs her name after the word *Best*. She too wants the goodness of life to be your companion. We are in this world to make a difference.

When I consider my relationship to the planetary constellation, I feel humble, for I realize my right relation to the rest of the world. I don't use that sense of humility as an excuse to give up and not try to make a difference. Actually, I move from the premise that if you are willing to let your light illuminate a candle in darkness, a star in the sky, or a torch along the path, you and the universe will be richer for your offering.

One aspect of astrology that I have found comforting is the concept of seasons. Astrologers teach the idea that each person's birth chart foretells and highlights different life stages. In my personal experience, I have found that there is a time and place or season for everything; that, good or bad, "this too shall pass." This knowledge gives me strength to persevere in the face of adversity and the wisdom to savor my quiet victories, for both will eventually come to an end.

Often, adversity or chaos is the handmaiden of progress. When something catastrophic happens in your life it may make you slow down, get a grip, notice your surroundings, change your outlook. How often have you found yourself running full tilt through your life, only to be stopped dead in your tracks by an unforeseen circumstance? Perhaps you come down with a serious case of the flu and you're bedridden for several days. Or maybe you lose your job in a corporate restructuring. Or a loved one suffers from a sudden or severe heart attack. Each instance, to a different degree, forces you to shift gears temporarily or perhaps permanently. I like to think of life's curve balls as wake-up calls, telling us that it's time to enter a new phase of our lives—ready or not.

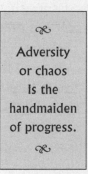

&

Adversity or chaos is the handmaiden of progress.

&

With interest I, along with many Atlantans, have followed the near-death experience of Dan Reeves, head football coach for the Falcons, during one of the team's best seasons ever. Suddenly, in the midst of all the fanfare, Coach Reeves had to have quadruple bypass heart surgery. It has become a life-transforming, life-saving experience. From the sidelines, he has openly shared with us all how it has clarified his life values. One of his most cherished gifts from this ordeal? His granddaughter emptied her piggyback to buy her grandfather a teddy bear so that he wouldn't have to sleep alone in the hospital.

Erik Erikson, the noted psychologist, used this notion to spell out the various phases of a person's life cycle: Each stage, he suggests, is characterized by a central task. If the task is successfully negotiated, a person moves on to the next phase of his life cycle, more complete and fulfilled. If not, the person moves on to subsequent stages of life but always remains troubled by the issues that he failed to come to terms with at the appropriate time. Some practitioners of the Hindu faith refer to those issues as "bad karma" and believe that this person will then have an opportunity and obligation in the next lifetime to face those challenges anew and to resolve them. If they remain unresolved, the person will encounter them again in the next incarnation.

My grandfather was a farmer, and he prepared his crops seasonally. He planted in the spring and harvested in the fall. He knew, as you must, the wisdom of the biblical proverb, "There is a time to sow and a time to reap." I encourage you to know this wisdom for your own life. If you find yourself feeling stuck, as though your life is lodged on a plateau, it doesn't necessarily mean that you're doing anything wrong. If you think about it, most lives progress stepwise. When you find yourself on your next plateau, rather than jump to change the circumstances of your life, take time to reflect on where you are. Perhaps you are in a sowing stage, and it's more important to keep planting than to worry about the harvest.

As important as it is for a farmer to work in tandem with the appropriate season, Grandfather also knew quite simply that what you plant is what you harvest. The proverb is revealing: "If you plant turnips, you will not harvest grapes!" If in your life you keep getting the same result, take a look at your life and see if there's a similar pattern to the steps you've taken leading up to the result. The answer is often not in the stars; more often, it's in the actions we take.

Act with integrity, for the actions you take are a powerful catalyst for the direction of your life and for those around you. If you behave in concert with your highest values, your purpose will be reinforced, your standards strengthened, your inner conflict silenced, your serenity deepened. Whatever the situation, you will always know the unconditional love and support of a true blue friend—way down deep inside yourself.

You are a star in ascendant. You must arrange your life so that you are constantly reminded of who you are. You now know to linger a little longer with yourself, to spend more time as a human being rather than a human doing. Make sure to introduce your outside to your inside (the two will be pleased to make the acquaintance). And look inward to find peace. If you do not do this, then you will find no respite in the world. These quiet times with yourself, far from being self-indulgent or frivolous, can help you develop your potential more fully so that you have more to share. As Gloria Anazaldua states, "I am playing with the world's soul, I am the dialogue between my Self and el espiritu del mundo. I change myself. I change the world."

Make sure to balance your professional, family, and community commitments with some "active rest." It is really not quite as odd as it sounds; engage in enjoyable activities and you will find yourself with a well-deserved "lighten up" assignment instead of a whole list of "musts." Do what you have missed doing and never tried.

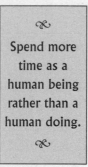

Spend more time as a human being rather than a human doing.

Take some emotional recesses. You are a human (didn't you know?) and even you can take only so much, go so fast, and turn in so many circles.

For just a moment think about your life progression: Remember when a home remedy cured everything, or so you thought? Remember when your parents' advice was your guiding light and shield? Remember when you were eighteen and you thought you were an adult, but then suddenly realized you did not want to be? Remember when your greatest obligation was to pay your monthly phone bill for $18.32? Remember when?

Do you remember when you discovered the power and presence of God or the One in whom you believe? Do you remember when you learned to drive, and bought your first vehicle? Do you remember when you started high school, college, and your first job? Do you remember your class reunion? (Time brings about a change!) Do you remember when you said, "I do" or "I don't," and started or ended a relationship? Do you remember your highest achievement and most devastating defeat and how you started all over again?

I do. I remember when.

> BE GENTLE WITH YOURSELF.
> *You are a child of the Universe no less than*
> *the trees and the stars. You have a right to*
> *be here. And whether or not it is clear to*
> *you, no doubt the universe is unfolding*
> *as it should. Therefore be at peace with*
> *God, whatever you conceive Him to be.*
> *And whatever your labors and aspirations,*
> *in the noisy confusions of life, keep*
> *peace in your soul. With all its sham,*
> *drudgery and broken dreams, it is still*
> *a beautiful world.*

> The Desiderata

Simply put, at the end of life, there will be a common denominator for us all. Engraved on our tombstones will be a birth date, a dash, and a death date. At the beginning of life you have no say. You have no input about your parents, siblings, economic status, neighborhood, gender, or race. At the end of life, you will not be able to "buy time" and postpone the inevitable. Your whole existence, short or long, is represented by the dash. There lies the cumulative effect of the many choices you make each and every day of your life. What will your dash show? Will it show the life of someone who chose to build, to contribute, to create, to lead, to act, to nurture, to think, to enrich, to cooperate, to care, and to love in a way that leaves a rich legacy behind? The dash is yours, yours alone. Cherish it. Let it burn bright. Remember its source. BEHOLD!

ACKNOWLEDGMENTS

In deep appreciation to my gifted literary agent, Caroline F. Carney of Book Deals, Inc., whose vitality is dwarfed only by her brilliance, for launching me on this first-time endeavor. I am also deeply indebted to the talented, professional, and truly inspired publishing team at HarperCollins, especially to Executive Editor Mauro DiPreta and Editorial Assistant Toisan Craigg, who believed in *A Is for Attitude* from the start and who have been unstinting in their generous support, enthusiasm, and good humor. Thanks too to Editor-in-Chief Joelle Delbourgo for her early support and wisdom and to the ace marketing, publicity, and sales team of Craig Herman; Joseph Montebello, Art Director; Paul Olsewski; John Wing; and Mark Landau. A special thanks to Richard Rhorer for making the book sales presentation and preparing the prerelease flyers that created the "buzz." I also want to extend my appreciation to all the people behind the scenes for their attention to the myriad details involved in publishing a book.

Many friends stepped forward and gave me early support in making this book a reality: dynamic presenters and bestselling authors Iyanla Vanzant, Les Brown, George Fraser, and Lawrence Otis Graham; visionaries and supporters The Honorable Andrew Young, Dr. Dolly D. Adams, Evern Cooper, UPS Foundation, Ingrid Saunders Jones, Coca Cola Foundation, Dr. Reatha Clark King, General Mills Foundation, Pat Harris, McDonald's Corporation, Valerie Daniels Carter, Burger King Corporation, and Felicia Hall, Nike, Inc.

A special thanks to the global family of the African Methodist Episcopal Church. A special thanks to Dr. Barbara Dixon Simpkins, National President of The Links, Inc., and to Dr. Norma S. White, Supreme Basileus, Alpha Kappa Alpha Sorority, and to all my sisters. A special thanks to John Crump, Esq., National Bar Association, and Dr. Carroll F. S. Hardy, Stuart Educational Leadership Institute. Thanks to the members of the media and marketing, especially Dr. Barbara Reynolds, Reynolds News Service; Monica Morgan, Monica Morgan Photography; Deirdre Guion, Niche Communications; Kiplyn Primus, Primus Marketing

Works; Nicole DeSane and DeSane Associates; and Patricia Anderson Ballard, PLA Enterprises.

And on the home front, many thanks to Pearlene M. Williams, my assistant, for her tireless hours in preparing this book and without whom my manuscript would still be in the computer. A salute to Charles L. Coney, my long-distance "computer whiz." A major salute to my family, especially my sisters Barbara Wilson and Verdie Anderson and their families, and always friends, Jarnell Burks Craig; Ken Glass; Barbara Williams; Attorney David and Lavonne Miller; Darryl Dyer, Esq.; JoAnn Brown; Suzie Bell; Ahmes Askia; Hal and Billye Elston; Ann and Moses Gray; Barbara McKenzie; and Debbie Williams, who have helped to thrust me toward the mark. A special thanks to my protégés whose achievements compelled me to remain steadfast: Honorable Hubert Grimes; Corey L. Wilson; Crystal M. Wilson; Courtney Beacham, J.D.; Stacee Bain, J.D.; Gregory Lacey, J.D.; Annette Minor, J.D.; Michael Watson; Donna Ballard; Stephanie Bright; Niquelle Cotton; Corey Craig; Nicole Williams; Lisa Cheatam Hayes, J.D.; and Anne Christine Haith. And eternal gratitude to Reverend Dr. E. Earl McCloud, Jr., supporter, friend, and significant other, who helped me to believe in and now realize this possibility.